Song of Songs

Song of Songs

歌中之歌

Watchman Nee

Translated by
Elizabeth K. Mei and Daniel Smith

CHRISTIAN LITERATURE CRUSADE

FORT WASHINGTON   PENNSYLVANIA 19034

CHRISTIAN LITERATURE CRUSADE

U.S.A.
P.O. Box 1449, Fort Washington, PA 19034

GREAT BRITAIN
51 The Dean, Alresford, Hants., SO24 9BJ

AUSTRALIA
P.O. Box 91, Pennant Hills, N.S.W. 2120

NEW ZEALAND
10 MacArthur Street, Feilding

ISBN 0-87508-442-7

Copyright © 1965
Christian Literature Crusade
Fort Washington, PA

also in:
Europe-Africa-South America-India
Philippines-Thailand-New Guinea
Pakistan-Indonesia-Japan
Caribbean Area

Revised Edition 1966
This Printing 1998

PRINTED IN THE UNITED STATES OF AMERICA

PREFACE

We are thankful to God that even in the world of today there are those believers who, drawn by the sweet love of Christ, do fervently long after Him. It is for such as these that "The Song of Songs" has a special ministry.

Spiritual fellowship with the Lord in the hidden, secret place of the heart is a very sacred thing and apparently something which should be sealed up. But in "The Song of Songs, which is Solomon's," God Himself has opened to us by His own revelation that fulness of this sweet and holy fellowship so that He may make us to know the paths of love and, at the same time, challenge us to walk therein.

This commentary is a composition of notes recorded by a brother when Mr. Watchman Nee met with several co-workers during their Bible study period. With the need of the present generation of believers in mind, this volume was first published in Chungking, China, in the year 1945, and again in Tsingtao in 1948. This present edition is being reprinted in Taipei, Taiwan. It should be clearly understood and appreciated, however, that the manuscript has never been proofread for correction by Mr. Nee.

May God use the message of the book to influence and help those who truly thirst after the Lord.

Taiwan Gospel Bookroom
January, 1954.

NOTE FROM THE TRANSLATOR

"The Song of Songs" often has seemed a mystery book to many. Some have wondered how it ever came to be accepted in the canon of Scripture. But spiritually mature souls always have regarded it as the heart of the Sacred Writings. The burden to present this commentary to the Lord's people arose in me because of the rich value the Song has in its typological interpretation, and because of the challenge which is arising against that exposition.

"The Song of Songs" has both a historical basis and a spiritual content. The spiritual content rests in the fact that it is an allegorical description of the marital union which exists between Christ and His Church. Mr. Nee prefers to think of the Shulamite bride in terms of the individual believer rather than of the Church as a whole, since not all who are the Lord's have a desire to go on to the realization of full spiritual affections. This invests the term "bride" with a meaning beyond the mere technical name, in that it sets forth the idea of full growth and maturity. A bride is not a baby, and bridal love is not baby love.

A theory which has never found much acceptance is receiving increasing attention these days. It suggests that the love suit is between an anonymous shepherd lad and the Shulamite maiden, and that King Solomon seeks to breach that union and so is a type of the World, against whose allurements the maiden proves loyal to her shepherd lover.

I am profoundly sorry to see this love-triangle view enclosed within such an influential translation of the Scriptures as the *Amplified Bible*. This seems most unfortunate, as it gives this modern theory a show of authenticity. Dr. Sidlow Baxter, in his *Explore the Book* series, thinks this interpretation is so artificial and distorted as to be at once discredited. We agree with Dr. Baxter.

Mr. Watchman Nee has been in prison for almost fifteen years under the persecutive Communist regime of China. There is no way to ascertain, therefore, whether there were any commentators to whom Mr. Nee owed an acknowledgment of help. I feel more than certain, however, that he had by his side that excellent work by Mr. C. A. Coates of the Brethren Assemblies.

Mrs. Elizabeth K. Mei, B.A.—one-time Supervisor of Public Health Nursing in China, and wife of the late Elim Y.L. Mei, M.D., Ph.D., one-time Deputy Surgeon General of Nationalist China—has been my co-translator. This accomplished Chinese lady made an accurate, literal translation of the words of the text while I myself made a much freer translation. These I then combined into the present, more-readable edition; hence I must assume full responsibility for this final work.

The translators would like it understood that the work is being sent forth solely as an edifying and, we believe, a proper interpretation of this most sacred and instructive portion of Holy Writ. Since Mr. Nee is in prison, we have no way of consulting with him about its release. But we believe there is something here which should be shared with the Lord's English-speaking people, in order to revive spiritual affections in these days of sad declension. With that motive alone we release it.

May the Lord, by this sweet Word of His Spirit, stir up many believers to become dissatisfied with a mere legal union with the Lord Jesus. May He cause all of us who are His people to thirst and to reach out for those full and mature affections described herein, which alone can satisfy His heart and best prepare us for His soon appearing.

Daniel Smith
1965

CONTENTS

INTRODUCTION

The first verse of Chapter One gives the title of the book. It is "The song of songs, which is Solomon's." The Song speaks of Solomon, and we are made to look upon him as a reigning monarch in great glory. In this, he is set forth before us as a type of the Lord Jesus Christ in all the triumphant life of His resurrection and ascension. When David slew Goliath and triumphed over that great enemy, his victory was a finger pointing to the victory of Christ through His Cross over all the power of the devil.

Solomon, receiving the fruits of David's victory, came to the throne as a king of peace, clearly pointing forward to the Lord Jesus, seated in the power and authority of His throne in heaven. The Song of Songs sets Him forth, then, in the capacity and authority represented by King Solomon. The royal fellowship into which we are directed, and which is typified by the Shulamite maiden (6:13), is in this exalted realm where our Lord, in His throne and His kingdom of peace, is so well pre-figured by this mighty monarch.

Here, then, we enter a realm where the battle with the enemy is already won. Peace reigns, and Solomon is a king who has received glory. Thus the book commences and permits us to behold our exalted Lord. Our relationship to Him, set forth in typical figure here, is not as that of Jonathan to David but as that of the Shulamite maiden to King Solomon. Jonathan loved David because of David's great victory over mighty Goliath, but the Shulamite loved Solomon for himself alone.

We see that there are some believers who love the Lord Jesus Christ simply because of the great victory He won in the Cross over evil powers. There are others, however, who have a fine appreciation of Him, not only for the struggle and victory of the Cross but for all that He now is in His enthroned life in heaven above. The Cross represents the Lord's battle to establish His kingly authority, whereas His heavenly life shows Him forth as triumphant and reigning. The Queen of Sheba at first only *heard* of Solomon's great acts. Later she *saw* Solomon himself upon his throne, and thereafter all her attraction was to the king himself.

In the same way, believers are not to love the Lord Jesus merely as Jonathan did David for conquering enemies, but, rather, as the Shulamite did Solomon, for His own worth. This book proposes to lead us, therefore, to know Him as the reigning King and to be by His side as the object of His supreme affection.

The Shulamite maiden's experience does not represent that of the collective body of believers but rather that of the individual. *Woman* in Scripture typifies a phase of subjective experience, and the maiden's longings indicate a single believer's exercise of spirit rather than that of the total corporate Church. It describes the beginning of deeper seekings after the Lord until such longings climax in the fullest fellowship.

The book's inmost heart speaks of spiritual communion. It is a book for the heart. It is not necessary, therefore, to inquire into how many parts it may be divided. The history it records runs like a thread and moves on continuously. It is not a record of nonessential sentences and odds and ends of stories from here and there. Its point of emphasis focuses upon the progressive phases in a believer's advance toward the Lord. It includes the experience of a whole lifetime and moves upward over many rungs or steps. The ultimate goal is that about which Madame Guyon wrote in *Spiritual Torrents** and Mrs. Jessie Penn-Lewis in her *Four Planes of Spiritual Life.** These are all of a similar nature.

The book addresses itself to those who already are regenerated by the Spirit of God and who are awakened to longings for a fuller experience of Christ. There is not the slightest mention of things pertaining to salvation. The emphasis is not on matters relating to the sinner but rather on those concerning the advancement of the believer. It does not address itself to those outside of Christ, but to the Lord's own people. Consequently, there are no instructions given as to how one may be saved, but it tells of the longings of a believer for deeper experiences of the Lord. It does not speak of faith, but of love. Love floats like a banner over the whole Song. Thus "The Banner of Love" may well be our ensign.

*A brief summary of Madame Guyon's *Spiritual Torrents*, and *Four Planes of Spiritual Life* are both now available under the title *Life Out of Death*, published by Overcomer Literature Trust, Poole, Dorset, England and Christian Literature Crusade, Fort Washington, Pa., 19034, U.S.A.

This is a book of poetry. It takes up the flowery language, the tempo, and the phrases peculiar to poetic utterance in order to describe spiritual events. In many cases attention can be given only to the mental concept and not to the mere statement of words. In the realm of pure devotion there is, of necessity, a limitation in words.

The Song of Songs and the Gospel of Matthew state two different aspects of the relationship of the Lord Jesus to the believer. Speaking of the matter of responsibility, the relationship is that of Sovereign to subordinate. This is the view given by Matthew in his Gospel. Speaking of the matter of communion, the relationship is that of husband to wife. This is the view given us in the Song of Solomon.

Finally, I would explain a few principles of exegesis. First, the exposition of each paragraph must have connection with the central theme of the book, which in this case is spiritual history. Second, the meaning of each sentence should, on the one hand, agree with the context, while on the other, it should be conjoined with the inner theme throughout. Third, when our Lord explained the parables of the thirteenth chapter of Matthew, He gave detailed commentary on some parts, but made no comment at all on other parts. Since this present book is an allegory, it should be treated likewise. Not all parts demand equal comment. Fourth, in investigating the terminology of names we should first find the intrinsic meaning of each word, and then seek further explanation by means of Biblical history. Fifth, when speaking of the bridegroom and bride the book constantly draws upon many other things as analogies. The main characteristics are all figurative, while the parables are all symbolic. Figures of speech are readily grasped but the meaning of symbolism can be understood only in accordance with the Biblical method and divine teaching. The nature of figurative speech and symbolism is often coincidental, but at times can be slightly at variance, and at other times altogether different in meaning.

However, we need not be concerned with such differences. We need only ask: To what does the passage point? Not infrequently, symbolism can express what a figure of speech can never depict. For example, in Revelation 1:15: "His feet like unto fine brass." That is symbolism—full of meaning, but not so easily understood as "His feet" alone, which anyone knows is a figure of speech for onward movement. Thus we must differentiate between figurative and symbolic speech.

THE SONG OF SONGS

THE TITLE (1:1)

"The song of songs, which is Solomon's."
Solomon composed a thousand and five songs (I Kings 4:32). Of all these songs, this is by far the most excellent, and consequently it is spoken of as "The song of songs." The most holy place in the tabernacle is called "the holy of holies." After the same style the Lord Jesus is called "the King of kings, and Lord of lords." This, in like manner is the Song of songs.

The book of Ecclesiastes, which precedes it, is an exposition of "the vanity of vanities" while this, in contrast, is "the Songs of songs." The Song which is Solomon's, therefore, is the antithesis of what is represented by the book of Ecclesiastes. Ecclesiastes speaks of a life *of* wandering; the Song speaks of rest *from* wandering. Ecclesiastes tells us that one cannot obtain satisfaction through knowledge alone; the Song tells us that man can reach satisfaction only through love.

Again, Ecclesiastes relates the pursuit of all things under the sun; the Song relates specifically to the pursuit of things in Christ. In Ecclesiastes we find that the wrong things are sought for and the ways of seeking them are wrong, resulting in the conviction that all under the sun is "vanity of vanities." But that which is sought after in the Song of Solomon is the right thing and the way is right; therefore the consummation is the supreme blessedness.

PART ONE (1:2 - 2:7)

INITIAL LOVE

This portion of the Song is the pivot on which the whole turns. The principles of developing spiritual life and experience lie herein, and this section may be regarded as a pattern. The lessons following this are not new, but each succeeding one goes deeper. All spiritual experience in this part is smooth and free from trouble. But the first offering of the heart and the first revelation of such things are not by any means fully dependable. They need to go through the fire of testing for strengthening. This first part, then, is but an image of spiritual experience; afterwards everything must be proved to make it a reality.

First experiences are not deep enough. Further degrees of experience with Christ will prove to be much more advanced and much more dependable. The experiences in this section may be said to be similar to what Madame Guyon in *Spiritual Torrents* means by "the Path of Light" and what Mrs. Penn-Lewis refers to in *Four Planes of Spiritual Life*. Each believer may confirm these lessons in his own personal experience.

INTENSE LONGINGS (1:2-3)

"Let him kiss me with the kisses of his mouth: for thy love is better than wine. Because of the savour of thy good ointments thy name is as ointment poured forth, therefore do the virgins love thee" (1:2-3).

The kiss longed for in verse 2 is not that of the father on the neck of the returning prodigal son, which represents forgiveness—a kiss which all who belong to the Lord already experienced.

The emphasis in this book is the relationship of love

16

between the believer and the Lord. Initial forgiveness of sins, therefore, is taken for granted as already past. The present book does not explain how a person is translated from the place of a sinner to that of a believer. It explains, rather, how a believer is brought from a position of intense need to a place of complete satisfaction. If we pay attention to this, we shall understand why the book begins as it does.

We cannot tell how much time may elapse after receiving new life from the Lord before a believer begins to feel desires for fuller measures of love's relationship. But we know that such desires do arise in the redeemed ones after having been awakened to life by the Holy Spirit. Subsequently a condition begins to stir within which expresses itself in thoughts of pursuing Christ for a more realizing and satisfying sense of His love.

Inasmuch as this maiden's heart is full of such desires these words unconsciously spill from her lips: "Let him kiss me with the kisses of his mouth." She is not disclosing to others whom she means by "Him," but in her own mind's eye there is only One whom she knows as "Him," that is, the One whom she ardently seeks after. Her former relationship with the Lord was a mere ordinary one which she felt to be most unsatisfactory. Now she longs for a far more intimate and personal relationship. She yearns, therefore, for His kisses, which would show His own ardent and personal love for her.

No one can kiss two persons at the same time, so this is a matter of personal significance. Moreover, this kind of kiss is not on the cheek like that of Judas Iscariot, nor is it a kiss upon the feet like that of Mary, but it is "the kisses of his mouth," which would express a most personal and intimate love. She is thus confessing at this stage that the ordinary or elementary relationship can no longer satisfy her heart and that she craves that direct expression of His love for herself which is not possessed by another—in other words, she wants to go much further than the ordinary believer.

This marks the starting point of real spiritual progress. It is an inward spiritual longing for the Lord Himself. The ultimate realization of His love and this quest of the heart with its fervent desires are eternally inseparable. If a believer has not this reality of a questing spirit created within him by the Holy Spirit—this dissatisfaction with the ordinary and this ardent pursuit of love's full end—then it is utterly impossible to attain to any intimate relationship with the Lord. These outgoings of longing desire form the basis of all fuller and future experience. If there is not this hungering and thirsting in the heart, then all that is here recorded will be but a poetic song and will no longer be to you "the song of songs, which is Solomon's." You will not understand what Solomon means by his song.

How is it, we may ask, that one is able to have such intense spiritual longing for the Lord Jesus Christ? The answer lies in spiritual vision. The Holy Spirit is evidently able to give vision to some which He cannot give to the average believer. To some, revelation is granted of the glorious Person of the Lord Jesus by which they perceive that His "love is better than wine." Because of this revelation of the glory of Christ such souls long for "the kisses of his mouth."

True indeed is the language in the heart of this maiden, "Thy love, Lord Jesus, is better than all the wine of earth— the sweetest and most excellent product which this world can achieve. The Holy Spirit has shown me that everything which makes man merry, or which inebriates, or which causes great elation of fleshly feelings, is not to be compared with Thy love. The things under the sun which men value most offer no comparison to Thy love. I have seen and I know. What is there under the sun, then, which can match Thy love?"

"Because of the savour of thy good ointments" (1:3). The Lord Jesus Christ Himself is the Anointed One. The Lord God by the Holy Spirit has bestowed that anointing upon Him. From the Spirit of the Lord He has received every kind of precious fragrance. Consequently, not only does God the Father smell the sweet fragrance of His holy life, but such also, as the loved maiden, scent the good savour. This is not something which she has heard here or seen there, but somehow, in a way far beyond the description of words, she has come to recognize the value of the loveliness and fragrance of His good ointments, by which she means the human graces of His divine life.

"Thy name is as ointment poured forth" (1:3). At the same time He has a name so sweet that it draws her to Him —"Jesus," meaning Jehovah the Saviour. That fragrant Name is associated with the comings forth of God into the midst of men—"Emmanuel, which being interpreted is, God with us." The sweet ointment of this precious Name has been *poured forth,* and we think of this immediately as related to our Lord's death. Yes! *The* ointment has indeed been poured out, and we scent the fragrance of His sacrificial love. This Name Jesus is thus truly precious, but who can fathom or measure the inmost fragrance of it?

"Therefore do the virgins love thee" (1:3). Because of who He *is* (the sweet ointment) and because of His precious *Name* (the sweet ointment poured forth in sacrificial love), therefore "all the virgins love thee." The reason for such loving is first because of who He is in His own Person, and further because of all that is represented in His Name. One cannot love service merely, nor yet love impersonal power. One can love only a person with a living personality, and here the Lord is that Person. This maiden loves Him for Himself and is drawn to Him by virtue of the greatness of His Person and the worth of His Name. When He was here on earth men did not smell much of that sweet fragrance, but since His ascension to the throne there are those who have done so enough to love Him reverently. Thus the revelation of the glorious Person of the Lord Jesus is not only what causes *praise* to spring forth, but what inspires men to really *love* Him.

"The virgins" denote "the hidden ones" of Psalm 83:3. The expressions are synonymous. The virgins are the companions of the spouse. They are equally chaste and are equally in quest of the Lord. Walking in this spiritual way, then, this loved maiden is far from being alone. Indeed, she is simply one of many virgins.

FERVENT DESIRES (1:4a)

"Draw me, we will run after thee" (1:4a).

Even though believers have fervent desires and are stirred to seek the Lord, yet they cannot but become conscious at the same time of an inadequate measure of strength for such

arduous pursuit. The power to pursue is not just the power
given by the Holy Spirit and deposited within us to enable
us to seek Him. It is not that alone. Rather, it is a revelation of the Lord Jesus given by the Holy Spirit as outside and
way beyond us, and thus drawing us to Himself by His own
beauty and magnificent glory. The drawing power of the
Person of the Lord Jesus Himself generates the pursuing
power in us. If the Lord draws us by the revelation of Himself through His Spirit, then the seeking after Him is rela-
tively easy.

If the Lord draws, then "we will run after thee." To *run
after* means a continuous desire. It is the attracting power of
the Lord Himself which alone creates the continuous power
to so seek and so run. This is something we must learn and
understand. No man of His own volition is able to seek out
and come into the realized presence of the Lord of glory.
When we were yet sinners we needed the leading of the Holy
Spirit, and only by His help were we able to come to the
Lord. Likewise, after we have become believers, we still
need that same help in order to run after the Lord with continuous desire.

Here also we see a believer's relationship to all other believers. It is *I* who am drawn ("draw me"), but it is *we* who
run after Him. It is *I* who am being led into the inner
chambers, but it is *we* who will "be glad and rejoice." Whenever the individual believer receives grace from the presence
of the Lord, then other believers cannot but receive favorable
impressions.

INTIMATE FELLOWSHIP (1:4b)

**"The king hath brought me into his chambers: we will be glad
and rejoice in thee, we will remember thy love more than wine:
the upright love thee" (1:4b).**

That the King had brought her into His chambers was the
answer to her prayer that He would draw her nearer to Him.
His chamber means His secret place, as in Psalm 91:1, and is
synonymous with a guest or bridechamber and thus expresses
a place of intimate nearness. If there is no affectional relationship, then one most certainly would never conduct
another into such an inner chamber. The King, therefore,

in this act of bringing the loved maiden into His secret place, was marking the beginning of an intimate communion with her and of special revelation of Himself to her. In that bridal chamber she unquestionably would taste a fellowship never known before and, incidentally, would see things she had never seen before.

The use of the word "King" here shows that before we come to recognize the Lord as the beloved Bridegroom of our souls we must first recognize Him as the reigning King. Complete dedication to His rule and authority always precedes a life of intimate love and devotion. The experience of full satisfaction in spiritual affections inevitably follows as a consequence to the step of complete dedication and utter committal. What we see here, is that the King has brought this maiden into His most secret place on the grounds that she fully recognizes His kingly Person and authority. Hence the King proceeds to give her the privileged experience of the inner chamber.

With expectancy, therefore, such believers as are represented by this maiden may lift up their heads in wonderment as the future unfolds before them. They know that the way of the future is limitless. As soon as the experience of the inner chamber begins, there is a surge of satisfaction in the thought of a life of love with the King, who is also a Bridegroom-Lover. Right well they know that God will perfect what He has begun to do in them. They say, therefore, "We will be glad and rejoice in thee, we will remember thy love more than wine." These are words which may be fully realized only in a day beyond the present, but having had the experience of the present, such believers are now filled with hope for the time to come.

"The upright love thee." A better rendering of the original would be: "In uprightness they love thee"; that is, they love Thee without mixed motives. The thought is that their love of Him stems from a pure heart and a good conscience, as in I Timothy 1:5: "Now the end of the commandment is charity out of a pure heart, and of a good conscience, and of faith unfeigned." It is upright love.

THE INNER CHAMBER (1:5-7)

"I am black, but comely, O ye daughters of Jerusalem, as the tents of Kedar, as the curtains of Solomon" (1:5).

Now to what class of persons does the phrase "daughters of Jerusalem" refer? This is a book in poetic song of spiritual and heavenly experience, hence the Jerusalem mentioned here most certainly does not have reference to the earthly but, rather, to the heavenly Jerusalem. These daughters are within the realm of the heavenly Jerusalem, by which is meant the system of grace. They must, therefore, represent those who are saved and who love the Lord Jesus Christ. Addressing them as "ye daughters" definitely indicates they are those who are born of God.

They seem to lack, however, the desire for that fervent pursuit of Christ which is found in the Shulamite maiden. They represent a lukewarm, beclouded, and casual company. Mr. Hudson Taylor once remarked: "In appearance they are saved—but merely saved, that is all." They are the Lord's people, but have not the degree and warmth of true, full bridal affections.

"I am black, but comely." Her first reaction to being brought within the inner chamber was a consciousness of her native blackness. Without her fervent seeking and pursuit after Christ, there would have been no possibility of her seeing anything of her true nature. She now sees herself as she really is. This consciousness of blackness is perhaps her first realization that such a condition is hers by nature. She may have known sins in the past, but this is a revelation of sinful nature. This black condition does not mean that she has been changed from something other into this, but rather it is a knowledge of her original blackness. It is what we all are in Adam. At the same time she has a realizing sense of the beautifying change wrought in her through the righteousness of Christ. Consequently, in addressing the daughters of Jerusalem, who represent those who have not the same spiritual intelligence and intimate affections as herself, she describes her own state in these words: "I am black, but comely"—black by nature, but comely in Christ. This comeliness denotes her acceptance in the Beloved and the transforming effect of grace upon her life.

"As the tents of Kedar, as the curtains of Solomon."
"Kedar" means "a dark room or chamber," so "the tents of
Kedar" point to her dark and uncomely exterior appearance—
her appearance by nature. "The curtains of Solomon" were
possibly made of fine linen and point to the righteousness of
Christ. Revelation 19:8 speaks of the righteousness of Christ
wrought out in the righteous acts of the saints: "Fine linen,
clean and white . . . the righteousness of saints." It is the
righteousness wrought in the saints through the work of the
Holy Spirit within. The curtains most certainly refer to the
curtains in the holy temple and are symbolic of that inner
beauty created by the presence of the Lord Himself.

**"Look not upon me, because I am black, because the sun hath
looked upon me ["burned me"—Darby's footnote]: my mother's
children were angry with me; they made me the keeper of the
vineyards; but mine own vineyard have I not kept" (1:6).**

"Burned" is in the indicative mood which represents the
act as an accomplished fact—e.g. "the sun has burned me."
By reason of the Lord's enlightment within the inner chamber, she has already seen that she is most black by natural
appearance. She does not wish, therefore, for other believers
to see this.

"Look not upon me!" This is an attitude very common
to early Christian life. We do not want our natural life to be
exposed at all. Thus, before being sufficiently dealt with by
the Holy Spirit, immature believers will tend to hide from
others. They do not wish to be known as they really are.

When, however, deeper steps with the Holy Spirit have
been taken, they do not desire to cover up anything of what
they are. It is at such a time as this that the maiden is willing
to be known before men as she is so clearly manifest before
the Lord. Hence she confesses, "the sun hath burned me."
In other words, the reason for my blackness is that the disciplinary ways of God have withered my flesh and made the
life in the flesh of no account to me.

"My mother's children were angry with me." Please note
that it does not say "my father's children" but "my mother's
children." Mother here denotes the principle of promise
which is founded upon God's grace, as in Galatians 4:26-28.
"But Jerusalem which is above is free, which is the mother

of us all . . . Now we, brethren, as Isaac was, are the children
of promise." The phrase "my mother's children" refers,
therefore, to all those who become God's children through
the principle and promise of grace—all who are saved by
grace.

The word "children," however, represents those who
merely cleave to a certain objective view of things and who,
without a corresponding subjective experience, remain immature in spiritual affections. They are such as take a strong
stand on doctrinal issues and contend more for objective
truth than inward affections. For the defense of such objective views they can become most violent and aggressive, as-
suming authority over the people of God.

But by reason of the Shulamite maiden's advanced devotion and the training she has received within the inner
chamber, a marked difference has become evident in her life
and service. This experience, not being understood by those
who view things in an objective sense only, draws upon her
not only the scorn and spite, but also the fierce anger, of
those described as "my mother's children." Her spiritual
desires for the Lord Himself draw out the bitter feelings,
even from those who are her kindred by grace.

"They made me the keeper of the vineyards; but my own
vineyard have I not kept." The first reference is plural—
vineyards, and it refers to works organized and arranged by
the hand of man. The second reference is in the singular—
vineyard, and this points to that work which the Lord Himself has arranged and assigned. "They made me the keeper
of the vineyards" signifies, therefore, her former manner of
life and service, which had really proved a distraction from
the Lord Himself. But having been enlightened by God,
and suitably dealt with and disciplined by His Spirit, she
sees the vanity of these former works. She had been doing
that which had been entrusted to her by man, but she had
been negligent of the work which the Lord had prepared for
her.

"Tell me, O thou whom my soul loveth, where thou feedest,
where thou makest thy flock to rest at noon: for why should I be
as one that turneth aside [wandereth] by the flocks of thy companions?" (1:7).

In the inner chamber the maiden had seen the vanity of mere external service. She recognizes that what the Christian needs is not so much a system of works but that unique place where the Lord feeds His flock and makes it to rest. Because of her need for nourishment she directs her attention now to where she can be fed, and because of her need of rest she looks for a place where she may lie down.

Henceforth, she will first seek food and rest. This rest means perfect rest of heart. "At noon" marks the element of perfection in relation to rest. "The path of the just is as the shining light, that shineth more and more unto the perfect day" (Proverbs 4:18). To arrive at noonday is to arrive at the high point of perfection of the day. When the sun comes to noontime it cannot become any larger to the vision. (It may be noted that our Lord's passion began at noon.)

"For why should I be as one that turneth aside by the flocks of thy companions?" These companions are companions of the Lord, but the flocks are not the flocks of the Lord. They are, rather, the flocks of His companions—companies of people who follow men of God rather than being gathered to the Lord Himself. "Turneth aside" denotes a state of being confused or ashamed—a state resultant from such a following. The maiden is still outside all that is represented by His flock, so she cries appealingly: "Where, after all, Lord, do you feed your flock and make your flock to rest— where, O where, can I find satisfaction? At this moment I am searching for food and rest for my soul, but I find them neither in the east nor in the west. Having been merely alongside the flocks of thy companions has made me a poor wandering soul—ridiculed and criticized! O Lord! would you not tell me these things?"

THE KING SPEAKS (1:8-11)

Within the inner chamber the Shulamite has come to see three things: first, she is black in Adam and comely in Christ; second, by reason of the Lord's dealings with her she realizes the vanity of her former fleshly and external works of service; and, third, she recognizes her need for spiritual food and rest. At this instant, therefore, the King responds to her diligent seeking, commends her, and gives her His promise.

There then follows the King's reply:

"If thou know not, O thou fairest among women, go thy way forth by the footsteps of the flock, and feed thy kids beside the shepherds' tents" (1:8).

The King addresses her as "the fairest among women." She is the one of greatest attraction to Him because of her capacity to appreciate Him. "If thou know not" is spoken in a tone which almost carries reproach, implying she ought to have known but has been taken off the path by attending to the works of others. But "if thou know not, ... go thy way forth by the footsteps of the flock."

These footsteps of the flock may indicate, on the one hand, the footprints of those believers of today who stand in the truth and position of the one flock. In other words, they stand on the true ground of the Church and are gathered unto the Lord alone; for although many today are the Lord's sheep, they may not yet have the flock consciousness—one flock, one shepherd—since they have no light concerning the real Church of Christ. The King in addressing His loved maiden tells her it is in such a place that she will find what she is seeking in the way of food and rest.

On the other hand, the text may be pointing toward all those departed saints through the centuries of time who found their own full satisfaction in Christ alone and suggesting that she may find it in the same way in which they found it. "The footprints" speak of vital experience. There is need on her part for movement into this experience of really finding the living presence of Christ, and of careful discrimination as to what such experience is.

The word "feed" in the text is the same as "to shepherd" —such works as a shepherd would do when he leads his flock to security, satisfaction, and repose. "Kids" does not mean sheep, since she herself is one of His sheep and these are *"her* kids." Neither do they point to the flock, since she herself has not yet reached that flock consciousness. The term indicates lambs; that is, those much less mature than herself and for whom she has some responsibility. "Feed thy kids beside the shepherds' **tents"** is an expression of apprehension that in her own quest for soul satisfaction and in being taken up with her own living needs she may neglect her duties to younger and more immature ones, and even close the door upon them.

Our attention here focuses on service and warns that in seeking for Christ in fuller measure for herself, the duty to younger and more immature ones must at the same time be met so as to avoid an exclusive attitude toward them. The mere betterment of oneself may become a peril to those pursuing higher states of spiritual affections. In other words, her food and rest in Christ may even come by way of caring and feeding for the lambs and will not be found if she neglects that service of love.

"Shepherds" is plural and denotes the under-shepherds, those who shepherd under the direction of the Lord. These are they who love Him and care for His flock. Their tents or booths, also in the plural, indicate the companies where such shepherds have the oversight. The Lord's intention, then, is for her to be alongside His true under-shepherds, those who shepherd under the Lord's direction. She is to find a place among them and so provide for those young kids for whom she herself has some responsibility.

On the other hand, she is to discern the example of departed saints in the matter of dedication, faith, trust, waiting upon the Lord, and in seeking God's will with singleness of heart and fervent prayer. It takes a high measure of spirituality to do that. In the daily living of each common day, however, she must care for those believers who are less mature than herself, and so fulfill the ministry entrusted to her. The sum of the matter is that even in those times when one is in the greatest pursuit of personal blessing the duties of each day's service to others are not to be neglected.

Again, there is in this portion the King's commendation and promise:

"I have compared thee, O my love, to a company of horses in Pharaoh's chariots. Thy cheeks are comely with rows of jewels, thy neck with chains of gold. We will make thee borders of gold with studs of silver" (1:9-11).

"My love" here may be translated "my lover-friend" and "a company of horses" refers to the very choicest horses. (The best horses in the days of Solomon came from Egypt as mentioned in I Kings 10:28-29.) **Verses** 9 and 10 denote her natural beauty—that with which she had been endowed by nature and which Pharaoh and Egypt signify. She was born and reared in Egypt and came forth out of that land. Verse 11 tells of the work which is wrought by God upon her and represents the beauty which is derived from Him. These verses, then, speak of six items: the horses, the cheeks, the braided hair (rows of jewels), the neck, the borders of gold, and the studs of silver. Let us look at these one by one.

First, the comparison of the maiden to "a company of horses in Pharaoh's chariots" implies that which is best in the natural life. The spiritual thought in this is that a good deal of the accomplishment in her life was of natural energy and power. The horse, from the standpoint of its natural characteristics, was a symbol of speed in those days. The swiftness described in the maiden's movements is parallel to her running after Him (1:4), except that here her swift movements have a natural and not a spiritual source.

Second, the cheeks refer to her natural beauty. The cheeks determine whether a person is beautiful or not; and in the maiden they are figurative of a natural endowment of good looks.

Third, the braided hair, to which the "rows" ("of jewels" is not in the Hebrew text) refer, is that which enhances natural beauty. The hair is the symbol of natural strength. We can see, therefore, that the maiden had much in the way of natural endowments and, from that point of view, she seems to have been passably fair.

Fourth, the neck with its ornaments signifies a kind of natural gentleness. Alone, without adornments, it is a symbol of something stiff and unyielding in human nature—i.e. stiff-necked. But in this maiden the neck is ornamented, and this speaks of an acquired gentleness through careful training and breeding which is found in some genteel characters. The reference is to that which belongs to Pharaoh and gives the impression, therefore, of the wealth and power which belongs to nature. In these manifestations of the flesh there is much danger. Thus these verses compare the maiden to a company of horses or steeds in Pharaoh's chariots. She is swift in movement and has a good measure of natural beauty, talent, and strength. The comparison is made to point out that, in spite of the revelation of the inner chamber and a true quest for a spiritual life, one's natural endowments may come into much prominence in this very pursuit. There are many who make no progress in spiritual life simply because of the intrusion of natural movements. Beautiful, graceful, and fast-moving though the maiden is, as described in verses 9 and 10, yet these are all of nature, whereas only what is wrought of God can be reckoned in terms of true values and carry us to our true goal.

The next two items, in verse 11, indicate what God promises to do for her through grace. "We will" is the King's promise, and in the plural "we" the Holy Spirit is making reference to the Trinity.

Hence, fifth, we have now "borders of gold." Gold stands for that which is divine in character. In order for gold to be beaten into a braid (border) much time is required. Gold braid is a fine and delicate work and represents the life of God wrought out through the ministry of the Father, Son, and the Holy Spirit into a special manifestation. Indeed, "border" in the original text means something like a crown. It is a wreath—a golden-braided wreath resembling a crown. This crown of gold is to take the place of her braided hair of natural strength and represents the righteousness, the life, and the glory of God which is to make her comely with divine features in place of natural ones.

Finally, the studs of silver bring redemption into view. To emboss this crown of divine work with silver studs or clasps points to the foundational work of all spiritual values in Calvary's Cross. Inasmuch as the whole wreath of gold is substituted for a wreath of hair, we see how that which is of God has to displace all that is represented by the natural man.

THE MAIDEN SPEAKS (1:12-14)

The ever-abiding and indwelling Christ is the subject of these verses.

"While the king sitteth at his table, my spikenard sendeth forth the smell thereof. A bundle of myrrh is my well-beloved unto me; he shall lie all night betwixt my breasts" (1:12-13).

Solomon's table is a topic of special significance in the Scriptures. "And Solomon's provision for one day was thirty measures of fine flour, and three score measures of meal, ten fat oxen, and twenty oxen out of the pastures, and an hundred sheep, beside harts, and roebucks, and fallowdeer, and fatted fowl . . . And the meat of his table, and the sitting of his servants, and the attendance of his ministers, and their apparel, and his cupbearers . . ." (I Kings 4:22-23; 10:5). Such was the provision for "all that came unto king Solomon's table" (I Kings 4:27). It was rich provision and blessed with his own kingly presence.

"While the king sitteth at his table," may be said to represent what the maiden has in the enjoyment of the full abundance of the Lord's provision. This bounty may be divided into two classifications. First, there is food made of flour or meal substance. This signifies the perfect Manhood of the Lord Jesus—His own holy life. Second, there is food of meat substance. This expresses our Lord's accomplishments—His work and sacrificial death so that believers may have intimate communion with Him in His enthroned life. "While the king sitteth at his table" denotes the precise time when there is a partaking of spiritual satisfaction in communion with Him.

This is a time of real spiritual joy. Each time we come to the King's table the chief entertainment is spiritual food in order to bring us into intimate communion with Himself. We partake then of God's accepted and prepared sacrifice— that redeeming sacrifice so well-pleasing to God. (Thus in the Old Testament days His people could partake of the set-aside portions of the sacrifices for their nourishment and strength.)

But how are we to partake of this sacrifice which is so well-pleasing to God? When the Lord God looks upon the death of the Lord Jesus, He sees an atoning sacrifice which deals with all that we are by nature. On our part, when we look upon the death of the Lord Jesus, we must see not only a substitution for our sins but also the matter of our union with Him in that death. At His table of spiritual food it is a realization of this fact which causes the rising forth of fragrance and praise in us—"my spikenard sendeth forth the smell thereof."

If we fail to perceive the real meaning of this well-pleasing and acceptable sacrifice which is the source of all true joy in spirit, we can neither dedicate ourselves to the Lord nor ever praise Him worthily. But when we do see that what we enjoy is identical with what God enjoys, then our spikenard sends forth its fragrance, and praise flows forth. The outflowing fragrance of Mary's broken box of spikenard in the Gospel story was because of the recognition of the meaning of the Lord's coming death. The Lord Jesus gives all to us; we offer ourselves back to Him. Thus appreciation of *Him* precedes dedication of ourselves.

"Well beloved" in verse 13 may read "Bridegroom-Lover." "Myrrh" signifies suffering love for her and points in meaning to the Cross of the Lord Jesus. At the time of His dying the Lord was offered "wine mingled with myrrh" to drink, which is exceedingly bitter. After His death Nicodemus brought costly myrrh to embalm His body for burial, signifying that His death was very precious to Nicodemus. "Night" in this Song always relates to the time of Solomon's absence, and this, from the spiritual point of view, refers to the Lord's absence from the earth. In Scripture the two breasts of woman mean faith and love as in I Thessalonians 5:8. The maiden is saying, therefore, "I will hold Him near to me in faith and love during this long dark night of man's wickedness and of my Beloved's bodily absence."

Verses 12 and 13 thus tell us of the indwelling Christ held in inward personal affection. To sum up: The clause "while the king sitteth at his table" conveys the idea of intimate communion with Him. The condition of so sitting at His table implies on her part an open door—the opening of the inner door of her heart to Him. "Behold, I stand at the door, and knock: if any man hear my voice, and open the door, I will come in to him, and will sup with him, and he with me" (Revelation 3:20). If we refuse to open the heart's door, then there can be no sitting at His table for intimate communion.

Myrrh indicates His suffering love, which is most precious to the believer. During His absence from the earth it is necessary to hold Him in our dearest affections by means of faith and love. This marks the beginning of inward communion, and through an understanding and appreciation of Him as discovered in the inner chamber, a spontaneous dedication follows. A life of sweet communion commences, and life begins to send forth a rich fragrance. Only in such a manner can we cherish the suffering love in the death of Christ, and only by holding Him in this way can we follow a crucified Saviour.

To be clothed and adorned with Christ is the subject of verse 14, by which is meant an outward expression of Christ. **"My beloved is unto me as a cluster of camphire in the vineyards of En-gedi."**

Camphire is henna-flowers, which Jewish maidens used for personal exterior adornment. "En-gedi" was a place to which David fled and hid—a place in the wilderness. "Vineyards" means the place of grape vines. The flowers of the grape vine are hidden from sight, so that this place was one where no flowers were seen. To find a bouquet of henna-flowers in those surroundings represented a most unusual sight. Thus was Christ to His loved one.

The scope of verse 14 is wider than that of verse 13. The bouquet of henna-flowers in a place where flowers were not generally seen symbolized the uniqueness of the Lord Jesus. Myrrh in the bosom, as in verse 13, is invisible and points to Christ being secretly hidden in the affections. But when Christ has become her adornment, as in verse 14, she is clothed upon with Christ and there is an outward expression of Christ visible to the world. This represents the fact that she confesses Christ before men, talks about Christ, makes Christ as a sweet bouquet of henna-flowers to be seen in the presence of men. Thus she here expresses Christ to the world of men.

THE KING'S PRAISE (1:15)

"Behold, thou art fair, my love; behold, thou art fair; thou hast doves' eyes" (1:15).

The first reference to her beauty is for her encouragement. The second phrase praises her beauty because she has doves' eyes. The eyes of a dove are truly beautiful, and the thought in view is that she now has spiritual perception or insight which makes her attractive to Him. From the standpoint of function the eyes of the dove can only see one thing at a time, and this signifies singleness of purpose. "If therefore thine eye be single, thy whole body shall be full of light" (Matthew 6:22). From the time she received inner revelation she has possessed spiritual insight. Myrrh, representative of suffering love, she has already embraced in her heart, as we have seen in the previous verses, and this means that her heart is only and wholly for the Beloved. It is this which makes her so fair in His eyes, therefore the King praises her.

THE MAIDEN'S REPLY (1:16-2:1)

"Behold, thou art fair, my beloved, yea, pleasant: also our bed is green" (1:16).
The meaning is that He is not only very fair in her eyes but also most enjoyable in this intimate nearness. This is her reply to the King.

"Our bed is green." She now has arrived at that of which she was formerly in quest—rest, and restfulness in association with her Beloved. Here is not only rest, but care—shepherd care. Green pastures are beds for sheep; therefore to lie down in them is to have sweet rest. This is similar to Psalm 23:2: "He maketh me to lie down in green pastures: he leadeth me beside the still waters."

The before-mentioned sitting at His table implies a restful satisfaction, but the primary interest in that circumstance is spiritual food. Here His couch includes the satisfaction of having eaten, but its emphasis is on restfulness. If shepherds were not skillful, the sheep would do nothing but feed; but if the shepherd be skillful, then the flock both feeds and rests. Thus they rest and are also satisfied and do so in this sphere of earth, which is suggested by the green.

"The beams of our house are cedar, and our rafters of fir" (1:17).
Cedars are trees which are tall, stately, and strong. They point to the new humanity in Christ our Lord. Most of the woodwork in the temple built by Solomon was of cedar and fir (cypress). Cypress was the product of a place called "Death City," and such trees were commonly found growing

in the graveyards of Judea. They were associated with death and thus have reference to the death of the Lord Jesus.

It is in the realization of what He is in His life and death that the maiden now obtains rest. The green bed of grass mentioned in verse 16 represents all that is alive — all that has life in Him and all that is edible from Him. Here, then, is her rest. And her need for overshadowing care and love relies upon the qualities of His perfect Manhood and sacrificial death.

The two most important kinds of wood in Solomon's temple were the cedar and the cypress. In other words, they were timbers proved worthy for use in the construction of a habitation for God here on earth. God dwells between that which is represented by cedar walls and cypress floors — the walls of His own Beloved Son's new humanity and the ground of His substitutionary death. And the place where the maiden finds her rest is the same place where God finds it His pleasure to dwell.

"I am the rose of Sharon, and the lily of the valleys" (2:1).

This verse follows immediately on the 17th verse of chapter one. There is no break. The words are not spoken by the King, as commonly supposed, but by the maiden herself. They would be something ambiguous if spoken by the King, since in the next verse He speaks of her as a lily among thorns. That would be incongruous.

Sharon is a plain in Judea and the rose would probably be some ordinary flower or a rambling rose so common in the province. Most likely, this lily is not the potted lily, but the narcissus which lies hidden in the deep valleys and which is unseen by men, but visible to God.

She is thus viewing herself to be merely "the rose of Sharon, and the lily of the valleys." In view of the King's commendatory remark in 1:15, she responds in 1:16 by praising her kingly Lover for His beauty on the one hand, and for the rest she has found in Him on the other. Now, having proper views of herself, she confesses, "I am just a very ordinary person, yet cared for and loved by the Lord."

THE KING'S REPLY (2:2)

"As the lily among thorns, so is my love among the daughters"
(2:2).

The King implies that she is indeed a lily, but his classification of her is not that of a lily of the valleys but a lily among thorns. In this the King indicates that she alone of all mankind has the purity and simplicity of the lily while the rest of unconverted mankind are as thorns. He is thus placing her in moral contrast to all that surrounds her.

Thistles or thorns from the Biblical viewpoint speak, first of all, of the fall of Adam and the resultant natural life from him. The first reference to thorns is Genesis 3:18: "Thorns also and thistles shall it bring forth to thee." They grow of themselves. They spring forth out of an accursed earth without having been sown. In Exodus 3, a section of Scripture dealing with such, a flame of fire burned in the thorny desert bush, but the bush was not consumed. The fire and the light did not proceed forth from the bush, mark you, but from the presence of the Lord within the bush. God made use of the prickly bush but did not destroy it. This may have conveyed the thought to Moses that at some future time God desired to use him in relation both to Israel and to the Gentile powers, but only by means of what was to proceed from the Lord Himself and not from anything which could come forth out of his own natural life. It alluded to the fact that God does not on any account take up the capital and resources of man's fallen and corrupt nature as a vessel for His use, but only that which is derived from Himself.

Then, second, thorns point to that which springs forth from the natural life of man, the fruit of sin. We see this in the reference of Matthew 13:7: "And some [good seed] fell among thorns; and the thorns sprung up, and choked them"; also in Hebrews 6:8: "But that which beareth thorns and briers is rejected, and is nigh unto cursing; whose end is to be burned." Such is the fruit of the workings of self-will. Such exercise brings forth the fruit of thorns, and these must be burned up.

"My love" is a plural form. This maiden, remember, is not the same as "the daughters of Jerusalem." In this present connection the Lord is looking upon those who diligently seek Him as did this maiden, whose lilylike virtues are utterly at variance with that which springs forth from the sinful stock. "As a lily among thorns, so is my love among the daughters." She and the company who live in sin are very different from one another. All around her is that sinful life which has sprung forth from the natural life of man, but she is as one with pure faith and love — as pure as a lily. There is also in this verse a hint that one in real quest for the Lord will suffer pain, loss, and loneliness in the midst of the wicked environment represented by the thorns.

THE MAIDEN'S PRAISE (2:3-6)

"As the apple tree among the trees of the wood, so is my beloved among the sons. I sat down under his shadow with great delight, and his fruit was sweet to my taste" (2:3).

At this point she takes up a comparison between the King and sinners. The phrase "the sons," pertains to all that captures the heart's affections, and which provokes sensuous desires as in Genesis 3:16; that which becomes ruler over the inward life in the place of Christ; or it could even be a place to which the heart of man is drawn rather than to Christ.

"The apple tree" is no doubt the citron tree, which is a tree of lovely foliage whose leaves do not fall in winter. In appearance the fruit looks like a pomegranate but tastes like a tangerine with a touch of lemon—a golden fruit of rare fragrance. Hence "the sons" implies what springs out of the corrupt natural life, but her Beloved, Christ, is like this glorious tree—unique. His uniqueness has three aspects: First, His coming into the world—taking His place in our humanity, but also a place of great and high pre-eminence *over* the sons of Adam's race. Second, His overshadowing, which can never fail; this is the evergreen-leaf which affords shade and shelter for the spouse. Third, His fruit—for there are many which may be evergreen but which do not bear fruit. Thus her Beloved is pre-eminent in the stature of His Manhood and at the same time affords shade from the burning heat of the day and provides His loved one with food for her spiritual sustenance.

At a former period she has already given herself wholly to her Lord. This, then, is now her testimony. They are words spoken to Him out of her own lips. They are words declared to all men everywhere. She not only says that His love is as good wine, but in this word she highly commends that good wine and speaks out her praise of Him. At this moment, then, she realizes that there is no other person, nor any other thing in all the world, equal to Him—no one or no thing can ever displace her Beloved. Within the churches there may be schismatic groups who say: "I am of Paul, or I am of Apollos" (which is carnal), but for this maiden the Lord Himself now fills her vision.

"I sat down under his shadow with great delight." "Great delight" may be translated "rapture." Sitting under His shadow signifies a tremendous lifting up of spirit—an ecstatic delight in His presence which gives the feeling of being taken up in rapture.

"His fruit was sweet to my taste." The partaking here is somewhat different from that of being present at His table in 1:12. There the emphasis was upon the Lord Himself; here the fruit of sustenance points more to those things which His work and life have obtained for us—such gifts as righteousness, sanctification, peace, and the descent of the Holy Spirit. On the one hand, she is conscious of rapturous joy in His presence and, on the other, she enjoys in His presence that which He has obtained for her. Each time such believers taste the flavors of these good things they find in them an all-inclusive spiritual sweetness.

Chapter 1, verse 4 speaks of her as running after Him; 1:8 as following after Him; 1:12-14 as sitting down at His table, although the act of doing so is not specifically mentioned; and in 1:16-17, though once again no action is described, she is evidently resting in His place of rest. Now here in this present verse she is clearly and authoritatively spoken of as having "sat down" and as actually enjoying His presence.

In 1:16-17 she has already obtained rest, but here in 2:3 it seems proper to make a clear statement of her having done so and of all she had received in so doing. Chapter 1 verses 16 and 17, therefore, is history, while 2:3 is an account and testimony of the experience.

"He brought me to the banqueting house, and his banner over me was love" (2:4).

"Banqueting house" may be rendered "house of wine" and suggests a place of joy and gladness. She is brought by the King into it. It is His doing and this is the second time she has been brought by Him into sensible joys. This present sharing with Him of His pleasure and fruits is in some measure different from the satisfaction she enjoyed by being seated with Him at His table (1:12), partly because of the presence of other guests and also because it emphasizes more her own state of joy.

Having, therefore, experienced an initial dedication and having been taken through a deeper experience of the Cross, there is a fuller realization of all that the Lord had wrought for her and made available to her, and thus it is for her "a house of wine." In other words, being brought by the King into His inner chamber, as in 1:4, is for the purpose of revelation; and this being brought into His banqueting house is for joy—to feel the joyfulness of His presence. "His banner over me was love" suggests that the hoisting of this banner by her focuses the whole attention on love. It is a love relationship. Such a banner represents what the believer does, and is a kind of motto or ruling motivation of life. Our banner is His love and it signifies that all the believer does is with no other motivation than love for Christ.

"Stay me with flagons [grape-cakes], comfort me with apples [citrons]: for I am sick of [with] love" (2:5).

Because the Hebrew verbs are in the plural form it would seem that the maiden's appeal was meant to be general, not immediately directed to the King. She exclaimed, likely to the daughters of Jerusalem: "Refresh me with delicacies sweet and fragrant; for I am in a state of deep agitation because of the intensity of my love."

"Sick with love" is lovesickness, and is the equivalent of being exhausted with happiness. Such was the experience of the saints of all ages when they came into a full realization of the Lord's special presence. It is that which Dwight L. Moody experienced when he was so overwhelmed with joy that he felt he could not contain such torrents, and he entreated the Lord to restrain the flow. For the joys of His presence can surpass the limits of what we can contain. The capacity to enjoy the Lord must needs be of His enabling; otherwise it is all too much for mortal men and cannot be contained by us. The earthen vessel has no natural capacity for the Lord and His glory, and therefore enablement must come from the Lord in order to have the capacity for such pure enjoyment of His glorious presence.

Intense spiritual feeling such as this can produce physical exhaustion. In this condition the maiden sank back with delight and ecstasy, calling upon any around to support her. Her Beloved Himself answered the appeal, putting His loving arm around her and holding up her head:

"His left hand is under my head, and his right hand doth embrace me" (2:6).

The left hand under the head infers that she would turn to look up to Him but needs support to do so. The right hand embracing describes the natural way of embracing a person. The idea here is that of the protection and support of His love. The emphasis is not so much on supporting strength alone, but on that supporting strength which is derived from intimate association. In other words, there is need for His sustaining grace that she may be equal to bearing the love with which He embraces her.

THE KING'S CHARGE (2:7)

"I charge you, O ye daughters of Jerusalem, by the roes, and by the hinds of the field, that ye stir not up, nor awake my love, till he please" (2:7).

Roes are of the gazelle family; "my" is not found in the Hebrew text, but has been inserted by the translators; and "he" should read "she" (or, better still, "it"), which would fit the context better. This is the King, not the maiden, speaking; for to "charge," or to adjure or command most solemnly, is in keeping with the true characteristics and authority of a king.

This concludes the first part of the book and is a description of spiritual experience. It is the Lord's desire that His followers should find rest. At this present stage, the goal of such tranquility of spirit and general security may be said to have been attained. Coming out from the inner chamber and then being brought forward into the house of wine may be described as a very smooth journey. The Lord now wishes her to rest awhile.

"The daughters of Jerusalem" are those who are fond of ecstatic moods and given to meddling. Consequently, the

Lord, in His address to them, warns them not to stir up His loved one—that is, to stir up her emotions—because, like the roe or deer, she may be easily frightened. The King's solemn charge in this manner speaks of this maiden as a victim of lovesickness—exhausted by the exertions of devotion. In such a state she should do nothing but wait awhile. She is in the hand of the Lord, and He would not permit these others to disturb her.

The lesson here is that if you are prone to meddling in other people's spiritual affairs, not only is it without profit to them, but such interference tends to frighten them away. Such a one as this maiden needs to rest a moment until this period of emotional exhaustion passes. She should wait until she is stirred again of her own desires to seek further experience. Others who may imagine she is immature are not to try to help her nor seek to stir her affections with fleshly energies.

The lessons she has learned have now come to a conclusion for the time being. Devotion has reached a certain climax. Let all things, then, keep silence before *Him*. "But the Lord is in his holy temple: let all the earth keep silence before him" (Habakkuk 2:20). He, the Lord, is silently loving you. Zephaniah 3:17 says that He will rest in His love for you.

The summary of this first part of the Song is this: First, in this opening section she sees the value of the Cross, but not the full reality of the life of resurrection nor the power of it. Second, the peril in this first phase is that of being over-indulgent in a form of inward communion which leaves her exhausted. Third, submission to the Cross and the true meaning of dedication with its proper application to life is still unknown to her. Since there has been no real proving of her, she has not yet actually taken up the cross. She still has not walked far enough in that way which brings the testing of the cross. Fourth, still another peril is that she only realizes as yet how precious the Lord has been to her. In other words, she has only been on the receiving end of the fruits of the Lord's labor on her behalf, but has not yet allowed the Lord to claim the fruits of His labor in her. That is, she has the Lord but the Lord has not yet gained all of her.

In short, this first section is merely *Christ for me*. I am not yet wholly for Christ.

PART TWO (2:8 - 3:5)

FALTERING LOVE

THE CALL TO ESCAPE FROM SELF (2:8-2:15)

Nothing is said here regarding her sins and failures. Yet it is at this point that new steps need to be taken by the believer in the experience of the Christian walk. For defects begin to manifest themselves as we go on in the development of spiritual affections, but the mere recognition of them does not automatically reveal to one the steps yet to be taken into the full realization of spiritual life. There are four things to be brought to her attention now:

The *first* is the power of resurrection life.

"The voice of my beloved! behold, he cometh leaping upon the mountains, skipping upon the hills. My beloved is like a roe or a young hart: behold, he standeth behind our wall, he looketh forth ["looketh in"—ASV] at the windows, shewing himself through the lattice" (2:8-9).

In verse 8 she delights in hearing the voice of her Beloved. That thrills her. But though she takes pleasure in His return to her, yet she does not, as we shall see, heed His words, nor is she truly submissive to Him.

To regard the Lord as a roe (gazelle) or a young hart can only have one obvious meaning, namely, it refers to the inspired title of Psalm 22: "Upon Aijeleth Shahar" or "according to the hind of the morning." Bible students all agree that this points forward to the resurrection of the Lord Jesus Christ on the morning of the first day of the week. Morning is the beginning of the day and thus the resurrection of Christ is the beginning of new life. For the believer, spiritual life and experience all begin in that resurrection life. Here, then, the Lord comes again to her, in His activities of love for her, in all the freshness and swiftness of that resurrection life.

These verses, 8 and 9, converge on the living quality of Christ in that life. Mountains and hills in the Bible all refer to difficulties and hindrances. "He cometh leaping upon the mountains, skipping upon the hills" denotes that there is nothing so high or so formidable as to hinder or prevent His approach to His loved one. The Lord is the risen Lord. Christ is risen. He has triumphed over every difficulty and hindrance. They are things of the past now. He is alive at the beginning of a new day in which all obstructions are put under His feet. He leaps! All hindrances are removed.

In this section, therefore, the Lord manifests His power of resurrection life, moving with all agility toward her — addressing her in a living way. In her experience as described in the first chapter she did not understand these things. Though she had known the swift running of her affections to seek Him, yet His "leaping upon the mountains, skipping upon the hills" was something not understood by her. The Lord now desires to instruct her in this matter.

In view of the fact that she has been so close and intimate with Him, it is not difficult for her to recognize His voice. But here there is a very apparent hindrance to their moving together, namely, a wall between them. This wall encloses the maiden inside, but shuts the Lord on the outside. She does not seem to be the least conscious that this thing is harmful and detrimental to fellowship. Thus she calls it not "my wall" but "our wall," implying that it was a wall of both their making. Basically, the idea of a wall in her thinking would be something to enclose her unto the Lord and shut them up together and keep the world and what belongs to it on the outside. Within this enclosure she had experienced many days of joy and gladness with her Beloved.

This is a picture of those who are overly introspective and who constantly seek the Lord only within their own heart. This maiden could utterly ignore her environment without —the people, her brothers and sisters, even her daily duties, and certainly her trials in the world. She could shut them all out and return again and again within herself to enjoy the Lord and forget the world. Thus she knew only the sweetness of communion, but little of the power for service or the fierce struggle of spiritual warfare. On the mountain top Peter wanted to make three tabernacles and abide there (Mark 9:5). In the sweetness of ecstatic mountain-top experience he forgot the multitude of sinning men in the valley.

With this maiden it is the same. Within her wall, on the mountaintop of ecstatic love, were the Lord and she, but down in the world below were men oppressed by sin and demons. Surely she had also built up within herself a tabernacle or a wall in which she enjoyed the Lord for herself, but she could not deliver sinners from the power of demons, nor had she the desire to do so. In other words, her returning again and again to seek only the personal joy of the Lord's presence created a wall, and it was solely the maiden's wall. This is the peril of the believer who has learned much of the indwelling Christ.

From the spiritual aspect of things we do not infer that the Lord departs from the heart of the believer. Here in this portion He is *standing* rather than sitting in a position of rest. It means He is ready to move into action. Just as sitting leads into rest, so standing leads into activity again. Again, the Lord is outside that wall, and His desire is to move and lead His loved one to new scenes beyond the bounds of that enclosure where she loves to pass her days. The power of His resurrection life is demonstrated to her in His ability to leap the mountains and skip the hills. Consequently, He cannot be imprisoned behind her wall. He must move.

Now she must learn not to lay hold of the Lord from merely a self-enclosed position, but, rather, allow the Lord to guide and lead her away beyond such confines. She is not to use her own strength to hold the Lord but is to allow Him to lead her. She must learn to trust in the word of the Lord, learn to exercise faith, learn to follow the Lord as He leaps over the mountains and skips upon the hills. She must learn not to lean upon the mere good feeling of the Lord's presence within her in order to live in Him. God be thanked, although there is a wall on her side yet the Lord has furnished windows for Himself. If these are not large windows they are at least small apertures through which He can look and shine within that once dedicated heart of hers.

The wall is my "looking inward"—which is capable of actually causing me to lose sight of the Lord. But He has furnished windows for Himself, and through these not only may He shine within us but we may look beyond ourselves. The wall implies that when you shut the Lord up within yourself you actually shut out the world of men and totally disregard the desperate needs of all who are without. The Lord desires, therefore, to deliver this maiden from this state so that she may prove His presence with her regardless of the environment into which she may be brought. It is necessary for her to seek Him not only within herself but to recognize Christ in all the circumstances of the world outside. This is a far richer experience than merely knowing Him within the confines of one's own private sphere. The Lord is omnipresent. Andrew Murray has pointedly said: "The Lord's presence should not only be a reality in your prayers, but a reality in the factory."

What, then, is the Lord's attitude outside the wall? It is one of standing, waiting to move. But the believer who is ever looking inward and is interested only in his or her own feelings of happiness does not really understand the meaning of the Lord's attitude and purpose. His voice may well be heard, but its meaning is not comprehended. There needs to come to the believer in this state and at this stage a clearer manifestation of His spoken word. Only then will there be intelligent understanding of where He wants to lead us.

Next is the bountifulness of resurrection life.

"My beloved spake, and said unto me, Rise up, my love, my fair one, and come away. For, lo, the winter is past, the rain is over and gone; the flowers appear on the earth; the time of the singing of birds is come, and the voice of the turtle [turtle-dove] is heard in our land; the fig tree putteth forth her green figs, and the vines with the tender grape give a good smell. Arise, my love, my fair one, and come away" (2:10-13).

"Come away" of verse 10 means "Come away with me." Here the Lord is speaking to her very plainly. What He is emphasizing is that she must come forth outside of her own enclosed life.

This is not intended to disparage the sweet inner experiences of the spirit, or else the Lord would not have given such in the first place. But to persist in this alone would incapacitate her for any encounter outside. Any impact with the world troubles those who live too much within themselves, and it robs them of real peace. From this time on, the Lord wants His loved one to be with Him in "leaping upon the mountains, skipping upon the hills." Madame Guyon said in this connection: "Heretofore His presence was a question of place and time, but now His abiding presence is no longer a matter of place and time. In whatsoever circumstances you may be you can trust and believe in the ever-abiding presence of the Lord. Thus the believer is no longer bound or encumbered by mere inner feelings."

Since the Lord now calls her to come away with Him, He sets before her all of past experience and the facts which are before her eyes. "The winter is past." Winter is gloomy and cold and not conducive to growth. It represents a time of testing in which there is little to cheer. In other words, the Lord has already conducted her safely through the experiences of the first section with its various trials of coldness, darkness, and seeming death. It was He who manifestly brought her through these trials and used His living presence to make her forget them all. Therefore "the winter is past."

"The rain is over and gone." The rain here is not the refreshing rain of springtime but that rain which, because of a cold atmosphere, turns into hail or snow. The winter rain can shut you in and make it impossible for you to accomplish any kind of work. Consequently, the rain here indicates winter conditions upon the soul. (Note such symbolism in Genesis 6 and 7 and Matthew 7:25, 27.) In addressing her at this stage the Lord is saying in effect: "Those many testings and trials are now all behind you because of your living sense of My abiding presence." There are, perhaps, these two aspects of the winter rains: The first would refer to the rains as those early trials which a believer may leave behind. They represent the believer's cross. The second would compare the rains to the Lord's own Cross and to the fact that His trials are now past. One should not, therefore, continue to rivet too much attention on the physical aspect of our Lord's death.

The reference to flowers, birds, turtle-doves, and so on are an appeal by the Lord to His loved one to stand on resurrection ground. Verses 12 and 13 both speak of that abundant resurrection life which, like the spring, follows winter. Had winter not been mentioned first then springtime would only indicate a resurgence of activity. But because winter conditions have been mentioned, and spoken of as a symbol of death, springtime means much more than death—it means resurrection life. The Lord desires this loved one of His to realize that she must not repeatedly focus her attention on the death, gloominess, and witheredness of winter in the soul.

"The flowers appear on the earth; the time of the singing of birds is come." Flowers are adornments of beauty. Birds represent the voice of happy song. Flowers are on the ground, while birds sing their song in the sky. Flowers express art; birds give forth music. According to Matthew 6, flowers and birds are objects of God's special care, and they express a heavenly message. They manifest heavenly beauty and set forth very sweet praise—the true elements of resurrection life.

"The voice of the turtle is heard in our land." This is the turtle-dove and its voice of praise emphasizes love rather than sweetness.

"The fig tree putteth forth her green figs." The fig is a winter fruit which remains on the branches until spring. It denotes fruit which has passed through the winter of death and survived it. It is the fruit which we acquire through the discipline of the Cross and the hard conditions of severe trials. It is fruit carried over into the afterwards of richer experience in Christ.

"The vines with the tender grape give a good smell." We must notice that the vines here are in blossom, and thus they indicate that the life of the believer at this stage gives forth fragrance and shows promise of very much fruitfulness. Fruitage is assured because the vine blossom comes after the young fruit appears. Other trees may blossom profusely yet not bear fruit afterwards. But when the blossom of the vine appears, the grapes are certain, since they are already formed on the branches.

This then is resurrection ground. All that is of death has passed away. The boundless future of abundant life has come into view. By means of this bountifulness of resurrection life, the Lord is leading His loved one out of her winter conditions. She must no longer be drawn to mere inner feelings of happiness but, rather, express the power of His resurrection. It is the time for action—time for the lover of Christ Jesus the Lord to step forth and manifest His life to the world.

The *third* matter brought to her attention is the call of the Cross.

"O my dove, thou art in the clefts of the rock, in the secret places of the stairs, let me see thy countenance, let me hear thy voice; for sweet is thy voice, and thy countenance is comely" (2:14).

The maiden here continues telling of her Lover's words to her.

Prior to this, her eye is spoken of as a dove's eye; now she is a dove. She is thus addressed by the Lord as though in an ideal state—a future position which she has not yet attained; for if she were already within the cleft rock and in the covert of the steep places in its deepest and truest sense, she would be manifesting the full life of the Spirit. She has yet to know the Cross in this deeper and fuller way.

"The clefts of the rock" or "the rock that was cleft" is a manifest reference to the Cross of our Lord Jesus Christ and to the sufferings He endured there. The verse is calling her attention to the reality of her position in His death, for what she does know of the Cross at this point is very superficial. In this poetic utterance the Lord is scanning her measure of spiritual life and He implies that she ought now to pattern her life after that about which He had already spoken to her, namely, the fulness and power of resurrection life. In order to attain all He intends for her, the possession of resurrection life must followed by conformity to His death. "That I may know him, and the power of his resurrection, and the fellowship of his sufferings, being made conformable unto his death" (Philippians 3:10) — a verse which parallels this very section in Song of Songs 2:8-14. The Cross in this is a subjective experience of the inner life.

"Let me see thy countenance, let me hear thy voice." Our countenance and voice should not be manifested through any other place or position than from within the cleft rock. The countenance and the voice are to be fashioned, molded, and perfected by the working of the Cross. That which is spoken of in part one as the Lord's real satisfaction lies right here. Initially, there was, on her part, a complete dedication and a fervent desire to follow the Lord in the way of the Cross. Now it would seem that she needs to be branded with the mark of the Cross. Both countenance and voice need to be hidden in the cleft of the rock and the covert of the steep places. Most certainly the point of emphasis is the need for union with Christ in His death—union, that is, where His Cross must become our cross.

A very important truth is revealed to us here. We are to live the life of the cross experientially. In going through to the place where we are made "conformable to His death," His Cross must become our cross. Then, what others see and hear of us bears the mark of the Cross which crucifies all manifestations of the fleshly life. But in order to be made conformable to His death we must first know the power of resurrection, since only His resurrection life can pass through the experience of the cross and survive.

The Lord was hinting in these verses that His loved one appeared all right but that she was not free from superficiality. The full weight of the cross, the full scope of her consecration, and the full meaning of the promises—all were as yet not fully known to her. In this respect she still needed to enter the cleft of the rock and the covert of the steep places

"For sweet is thy voice, and thy countenance is comely." This voice refers on the one hand to prayers and on the other to praises. In the first section it was the maiden's desire and hope to possess the King for herself. Consequently, the King commented on the fact that her eye was like a dove's eye—having only one object in view. All her praises were praises of the King. We may say, then, that in the first section she was greatly impressed with the King, her Beloved, and let it be known. But the truth of the matter is that the King is the centrality of the whole experience and that she should live for Him.

In the first section she herself is the center of attraction, whereas now the position is reversed and the King has the central place. She is submissive and second to the King and should now concentrate upon satisfying the King's heart, since she already has the King for herself and has already found her own satisfaction in Him. It is not now a question of her adoring praise and her delighting in the King, but, rather, the King's turn to enjoy her, admire her, and love her. In time past it was Christ for me; now it is I for Christ.

The Lord thus begins to demand the fruit of His sufferings from her in order to satisfy His own heart. At this stage He hints that what He desires is that she should live for Him alone and thereby He calls her to a place in the cleft of the rock and into the covert of the steep places. This is what He wishes her to see.

The Lord is calling her to arise, to cast off self-life, to be delivered from mere sensual feelings, to break the shackles of this super-introspection. His desire for her is to receive the power of resurrection life and to exhibit to the world the clean and holy new-creation life given her through the Cross. This is not now the time to be in the house of wine. It is the time when she must move out and live for the Lord.

And why arise? Evidently to change the focal point of life. The thought is that from this time forth all those who are progressing in the pursuit of the Lord and who live in the world should have no other compelling purpose but to receive constantly the power of resurrection life and to live out before men the life of the Cross. This is what gives the Lord full satisfaction and is so well-pleasing to Him. In other words, Christian life is not a mere personal enjoyment for the individual. It is the satisfaction and delight of the Lord Jesus in all who are His own.

"For sweet is thy voice, and thy countenance is comely." This did not imply that there was any natural beauty or sweetness in her. The word means that her voice is sweet and her countenance comely only as she is found in the cleft of the rock and in the secret of the steep places. It is only so as she takes her place in the death of the Cross and her life is manifested from the high places. Because the rock is cleft she may hide there. This portrays union—being in Christ.

Going into the secret places means being fully and completely in His risen life. This is completeness of identity. Being thus united signifies complete oneness with Christ.

"The secret places of the stairs" or "the secret of the steep places" points to the ascension which ordinary men cannot reach. "For ye are dead, and your life is hid with Christ in God. When Christ, who is our life, shall appear, then shall ye also appear with him in glory" (Colossians 3:3-4). Stairs or steep places is interpreted by some as "ascension" and by others "inaccessible to mortals." Steep or precipitous places are very high and they challenge human endurance. They call for a steady crawling ascent. This differs very much from what is written in Ephesians of our position in Christ — that of being seated with Him in heavenly places.

But this ascent in the Song focuses not so much upon what position God has given us in His Son, but our approach into it and actual experience of it. The Lord is here demanding the life of the Cross in His loved one and a living expression of His resurrection life, for example, "Let me so hear thee, and see thee!" It is only as she realizes her union with Him in His Cross that He will be able to say that her voice is sweet and her countenance comely. The intention of the Lord's exhortation is a plea for her to be dealt with by the working of the Cross, to cast off all sin and all that is of the natural life. When all that issues from the old Adam, all which is natural, has been dealt with, then that which rises and remains will be of the new creation. It is thus that the sweet voice and comely countenance issue forth from the cleft rock and the secret of the stairs.

In these days our life is to be a day-by-day subjection to the dealing of the Cross and a casting off of all that is in Adam. At the present time it is not ours to go forth to obtain resurrection life but rather to put off all that life which is of Adam. Every benefit which issues from resurrection life we already possess. But at the same time we bear with us much that issues from Adam and which hinders the enjoyment and expression of the other. Thus the question of today is not how much do we possess of Christ, but the question rather is how much have we lost of Adam.

The *fourth* matter brought to her attention is the removal of hindrances.

"Take us the foxes, the little foxes, that spoil the vines: for our vines have tender grapes" (2:15).

Since these words were spoken by her Beloved, they must have reference to the blossoming vines spoken of by Him in 2:13, vines bearing the fruit of spiritual life. "Take us [Let us catch] the foxes" is very much a command. Big foxes go after the fruit of the vine, but little foxes break the tender vine branches.

Though damage may be done by big foxes, you may still have a chance to bear some fruit, but with the damage done by little foxes the chance of fruitage is almost destroyed. Unless we are very watchful, the life of the Cross prior to resurrection and the experience of ascension after resurrection can be completely spoiled by little foxes.

"Our vines have tender grapes." The grapes being on the vine, the blossoms were out, as these appear after the fruit is formed. Thus the blossom gives forth sweet fragrance when the fruit is young and shows the initial step toward a full and complete life in Christ. The beginnings of the manifestation of resurrection life and ascension life are in embryonic stage, but all very sweet. The fruit of life is full of promise. If unwatched or unguarded now, the little things can ruin it all.

What are the little foxes? Every small appearance of the old life — a habit, a retrospective look — such are the little foxes. They are not necessarily grave sins. We are told in Ecclesiastes 10:1: "Dead flies cause the ointment of the apothecary to send forth a stinking savour: so doth a little folly him that is in reputation for wisdom and honour." Little foxes hide themselves behind the vines. If unnoticed they can easily destroy the vine. Subjectively speaking, the first step of hindrance is in the matter of following the Lord. Little foxes do their damage and cause conditions of fruitlessness usually before the resurrection life in Christ is strongly established within. We must therefore beware of the little foxes.

In dealing with all small problems — the little foxes — the loved one cannot withstand them singlehanded, nor can the King do it alone. There is need for co-operation. He is asking her that they war against these things together.

FAILURE AND RESTORATION (2:16-3:5)

"My beloved is mine, and I am his: he feedeth [his flock] among the lilies" (2:16).

The loved maiden has now come to realize and understand the King's attitude toward her and has heard His voice and, having taken a retrospective glance at her complete union with Him, she thus expresses her joy. She turns her head to review the experiences of what has been hers in the first part of the Song. There is one matter which has brought her heart satisfaction; namely, her Beloved is hers. The Beloved's attitude toward her is known to her with crystal clarity. He loves her dearly. She also knows that she belongs to the Beloved One. But He was not at this stage her sole point of focus. She turns her head to review past experiences and in this she herself becomes the center of attraction to herself. (Later on, in chapter 6:3, we see the King as the center of attraction, even though she still has an emphasis on herself, but in chapter 7:10 the King is the sole focus of attention, and it is there that she forgets herself altogether.)

Her testimony in this verse is doubtless true, nevertheless it is quite beside the point. What a most disappointing answer it is to all that the Lord has spoken! The question is not whether what she said was well spoken or not, but rather, did the words of her Beloved really register? Did she rise and respond to His "Come away"? As a newly dedicated person she knew only too well what comprised the Lord's claim upon her, but she could not forget all that the Beloved was to her personally. She persisted in being the center of attraction, instead of realizing that her Lord is the center of all things. At this stage, however, she possesses these strong feelings which assure her that she herself belongs to the Beloved. That was the kernel of her happiness — herself the object of His love.

"He feedeth among the lilies." Though she is here speaking about the question of His service, yet there is no emphasis on how He deals with His flock. She simply stresses the relation between the Lord and the lilies — the lilies being those people with dedicated and pure hearts toward the Beloved. They are the planting of the Lord Himself—the Lord's peculiar workmanship because of so great measure of response to Him. (Psalm 45 is the song of the lily or pure love.) Among such a company the Lord really feeds His flock. Her implication is: "I'm His lily, so the Lord really loves me in a special way. I have the Lord Himself to attend me, and I am fully satisfied." It is the peril of mature souls. That which she emphasizes is what He is to her. Her attention is still upon herself — feeling she is a special object of His love. But judging from her own remarks she had failed to respond to the present call and demands of His love, and thus He was not fully satisfied with her.

"My beloved! . . . Until the day break, and the shadows flee away, turn, my beloved, and be thou like a roe or a young hart upon the mountains of Bether" (2:16-17).

Here, then, she admits there were shadows in her life, and thus she confesses her failure to meet His demands and to satisfy His heart. She recognizes also that the complete union with the Lord is somewhat theoretical and far from realized. She has known the sound of His voice, the call of the Cross, the demands for a heavenly overcoming life, and the importance of manifesting the power of resurrection; but there is now a realization that she had come short of it all. She is not prepared to go with Him although she wants Him to come to her.

She therefore said to the Beloved: "Wait until the shadows flee away — then I'll come with You!" She longs for a new day — hoping for a day when He will return to her — for a day when the shadows shall pass away. For this cause she would have the Beloved One turn His head. "Turn, my beloved!" This word "turn" discloses two aspects of her inner life.

First, although spiritual affections are present, she has fallen behind Him, and He is not really present with her since she had not responded to His call to leave her enclosed wall and come away with Him.

Then, second, it discloses the fact that though she was not refusing the presence of her Beloved, yet she was insisting upon having Him in her circumstances and behind her wall for her own personal comfort. She was looking again for mere comfortable feelings of inner satisfaction which she had known in the past, but she was actually failing to respond to be with Him in His circumstances of "leaping upon the mountains, skipping upon the hills." Her chief joy and the object of all her seeking were, doubtless, feelings of inward happiness, precluding the exercises of resurrection life. She was still lacking that persistent on-going of faith in the spirit which would follow the Lord whithersoever He would go and wheresoever He would be. This remains a lesson yet unlearned by her and a matter she could not at this stage perform.

It is here that she experiences a very significant revelation — that she is not necessarily where the Lord is. Hitherto, the only place she could enjoy His presence was within this wall of her own feelings. To her, this was the only place and the best place to enjoy the Lord, and this therefore was the highest pinnacle of her life. She still did not know the priceless experience of the Lord's omnipresence. Leaping upon the mountains could be her experience with Him and skipping upon the hills could be realized amidst her daily chores, both in the home and in the world. She was aware of the fact that He was inviting her to move with Him in His goings, yet she had no desire to go with Him. With no deep comprehension of the anguish of separation, which is the meaning of the mountains of Bether, her nonchalant remark was a mere "Please return to me soon!" She would have Him come back to her, although she is not prepared to go out with Him.

What she missed by not going out with Him in His goings is lamentable! She neither asks for strength that she may be led out with Him nor does she seek a way out beyond the mountains of Bether (separation). She would rather endeavor to force Him back into her circumstances and have Him enclosed with her in her own little circle for selfish comfort.

But things turned out entirely different from what she expected. When the Lord went away from her, He thus deprived her of the pleasant inner feelings of His presence.

In truth, the Lord never forsook her, but the withdrawing of His sensible presence produced feelings of desertion in her. The method of teaching employed by the Lord for her spiritual advancement plainly taught her that if she insisted on His living presence being drawn into her circumstances of a purely soulish character, then she would lose the comfortable and sensible feelings of His spiritual presence.

In verse 2:17 we are not told the length of His absence, but it is certain that if we do not abide in Christ and move with Him in His circumstances, then we cannot become conscious of His presence in our emotional feelings. On the other hand, if we do abide in Christ by faith, we may not necessarily feel His presence in our emotional feelings. This is precisely true of many believers who, after experiencing many sweet feelings of His presence, discover later, without knowing the reason why, that it is impossible to renew that unique phase of experience again. You see, when the Lord's highest purpose is thwarted by your lack of response, then your desire for sensible feelings cannot possibly be attained. Without a new encounter with Him, and without receiving new grace from Him, you lose what you once possessed. You may suppose that you are still living in the experience of 1:13, whereas in reality you are in the sad condition of 3:1. Both verses contain the word "night." In 1:13 she had her Beloved in embrace betwixt her breasts throughout the night. Wonderful! — but during a following night, unknown to her, He had made His departure.

This was for no other reason than that she treasured most of all her own sensible feelings of the Lord's presence, and because she preferred having Him in hiding behind an inclusive wall of her own, in order to maintain those feelings. She deliberately shut herself out from any environment in the world, and this at the expense of having the Lord labor there alone without her help. The resultant state was one of incomplete union with her Beloved, both in His interests and service. The Lord, therefore, had to remove these sensible feelings of His presence from her, so that she could be made to realize a new attraction in Him and be drawn out in quest of Him. This is the maiden's first awakening to really going out to the Beloved in *His* circumstances.

"By night on my bed I sought him whom my soul loveth: I sought him, but I found him not" (3:1).

"Night" here is in the plural. The Beloved was gone many succeeding nights. This, indeed, passed her understanding. But we see that the Lord, capitalizing on her love for feelings of communion with Him, draws her out to pursue that which He desired of her. Having lost these sensible feelings of His presence, she deemed she had lost Him altogether. How foolish and infantile! Unacquainted with the Lord's high intention for her, she set forth supposedly to seek Him whom she really loved. In 3:1-2 she thrice speaks of her seeking Him and really thought she was doing so. "I sought him whom my soul loveth." But actually she was not seeking *Him,* but only a recovery of her own sensible feelings of His presence. Nevertheless, she was seeking!

"I will rise now, and go about the city in the streets, and in the broad ways I will seek him whom my soul loveth: I sought him, but I found him not" (3:2).

The "arise" of the prodigal in Luke 15:18 was toward the Father; here it is the mature believer's rise toward the Son. We see in 3:1 that her seeking of Him was in her bed, implying that she had not made the slightest move out of her condition. She was seeking in the wrong place; for as long as we remain in our bed we shall never find Him.

We recognize that our first step in Christian experience is knowing the Lord on the Cross. The second step in advancing spiritual experience is possessing Christ as an indwelling Reality, and this brings with it sensible feelings of communion and the experience of being conducted into His secret chamber and into His banqueting house. The third step is abiding constantly in Christ wherever He may lead, and in these circumstances there are no bounds of place, space, or time.

This loved maiden had doubtless taken the first two steps, but had not yet taken the third step. Her bed — a place of rest — afforded rest. It was *hers,* not His. And the Lord was disturbing her rest, since it was not a proper spiritual rest. As one who in the first place knew no rest, she had graciously been led by the Lord into His rest, saying in 1:16-17: "our bed is green. The beams of our house are cedar, and our rafters of fir." But now, as one who had experienced that rest already, the Lord wanted to take her into the experience of "leaping upon the mountains, skipping upon the hills" with Him. In order to bring her into that state He makes her feel His absence in the place of her unworthy rest.

She now realizes her faith had failed in His goings and that because of it her pleasant feelings had gone. She was, therefore, determined to rise up. "I will rise now and go about." This simply implied a willingness to move out of her present condition of false rest. The Lord was teaching her that this condition is not the place of true rest nor is it the time for rest in relation to the world. She needs to be delivered from that kind of rest and begin to learn the deeper rest found in following the Lord in all His circumstances through the power of His resurrection life.

Hence she said that she would arise and "go about the city in the streets" (in those days the city meant Jerusalem, and it points to everything which belongs to the heavenly realm). She desires to seek out Christ Himself from amidst heavenly facts, heavenly things, and heavenly beings. Perhaps she had spent much time studying the many doctrines in the Scriptures, examining many books of human origin, and attending the gatherings of spiritual people. She had done all these; but, not stopping at them, she arose and went about the streets of the city and the broad ways, ever seeking the Lord Himself.

This is the first evidence of reviving affections. These places were in the city where people had fellowship and communication. They represent the means of grace, since the Lord Himself is in these ways. In other words, the Lord's people commonly employ ways and means for fellowship and for receiving grace and blessing. Thus she, too, resorted to the same means, which might include confession of sin, repentance, prayer, fasting, meetings with saints for fellowship, faith, or trust; yet her use of these means failed to reveal to her the Lord Himself.

She had now begun to lift her head and leave her bed of ease and learn the value of fellowship with others of God's people — thus moving in God's appointed way. She no longer attempts to cover up her need, or to save her face by pretense; also she no longer stresses mere external works to hide the inward inadequacy. She learns to mingle with others of God's children in order to gain help for her spiritual dilemma. Hitherto she had accustomed herself to only one way of receiving grace, namely, her own bed of ease. Now she would stir herself, walk the streets of the city, and enter the busy places where believers congregate in gatherings; even though, thus far, she had failed to find Him there. Yet He did not seem to be beyond the limits of the city — the realm in which she was — for yet a little while and she was to meet Him. The problem at this time was simply one of time, of patient seeking over a period.

"The watchmen that go about the city found me: to whom I said, Saw ye him whom my soul loveth?" (3:3).

The watchmen were a group of men who guarded the city in the darkness. They were men chosen and entrusted by God to guard the souls of His people, as Hebrews 13:17 states. "Obey them that have the rule over you, and submit yourselves: for they watch for your souls, as they that must give account, that they may do it with joy, and not with grief: for that is unprofitable for you." These watchmen that went about the city were well taught in spiritual subjects. Some of them may even have given a helping hand to this maiden in times past. She did not now particularly seek them, but because of their office and the trust vested in them by the Lord, they met and encountered her. And, reflecting within herself, she thinks that perhaps they could help her now in searching for Him whom her soul loved.

The watchmen, however, could do no more than point the way to Him or give right instructions. To meet the Lord Himself, you still must reach out yourself for the Lord. No watchman can do this for you. You see, when you look for watchmen you may not be seeking for the Lord. Every seeking soul must have dealings with the Lord Himself and likewise be dealt with by the Lord alone. Watchmen may be helpful at times, but at other times are not. If it is true that you are being dealt with by the Lord and you turn with greater confidence to watchmen, then you will come away with continuing disappointment and dissatisfaction. You must realize that the way which leads to Him whom the soul loveth is, paradoxically, to depart from the watchmen.

Perhaps you, too, are like this loved maiden. Notice, then, it was after passing them and going on a little farther alone that she found Him whom her soul loved. Going about the city streets and meeting for fellowship is doubtless necessary, but it did not actually lead her to the Lord. The Lord wanted her to walk in a spiritual, solitary way. Thus in vital experience, the watchman's assistance may be of no avail, or may have to come to an end, in the ultimate goal of finding the Lord.

"It was but a little that I passed from them, but I found him whom my soul loveth: I held him, and would not let him go, until I had brought him into my mother's house, and into the chamber of her that conceived me" (3:4).

We may ask what significance there was in this present encounter with her Beloved? There is no indication that her going about the city was the correct procedure, or that her walk in the street was proper; nor does it say that her confession of failure before the watchmen was complete and approvable. Most assuredly she had many lessons to learn. Not only did she have a vital place in the Lord's heart, but also she was as one held in His hand. However, this does not mean that she had reached the mark of perfection in once again meeting the Lord. But it does indicate that the Lord knew just how much testing she could bear at this particular stage. Though yet imperfect, nevertheless the Lord was pleased to be found of her because of her indefatigable heart search for Him. This then brought her present experience of trial and testing to a conclusion.

After a short period of time she would be led farther on the way to spiritual maturity, which still lay before her. In one whose condition is still one of incomplete union — as indicated in her search for Him — it is difficult to escape many impurities and imperfections, but at this time the Lord is not dealing with her on these issues. In these early steps of spiritual experience the Lord was willing to allow that those who seek shall find, in spite of the fact that her seeking lacked a certain spiritual quality. Here, as Ezekiel says (Ezek. 47), He brought her through a measured water. It seems as though the Lord had measured this portion and allowed His loved one to pass through. This part of the way was according to His limited measure for her present condition.

"I held him and would not let him go." Now she is sure that she has found Him whom she had lost. She fain would now hold Him firmly lest she lose Him as she did before. This time she must be alert and watchful to keep Him. Although she realized that she should come forth and be with the Lord where He is in His circumstances, yet she still wants Him in her feelings, while admiring Him in her heart. The lesson of coming forth unto Him has not yet been learned. She has risen but has not gone forth with Him. She has not yet learned to give the Lord freedom to come and go as He pleases. She does not know that it is impossible to have both the true life of faith and permanent lively feelings of the Lord's presence.

The maiden wants to grasp Him and hold Him. She still does not realize that in order to have Him present in our feelings we must allow Him liberty to come and go as He pleases. When it does please Him, we may be given comfortable feelings of His presence; but when it does not please Him to do this we must give Him liberty, and not hold on to Him and all He is by sheer obstinacy. She still does not understand this but regards His presence in her feelings as the supreme good. There is no true understanding of the way and life of faith, so she clings to Him and will not let Him go. However, when we hold on to the Lord by carnal means, it is but an indication that this carnal self must be dealt with. Spiritual seeking will give the Lord liberty as He pleases. Soulish seeking will reckon on selfish interests, even though what is sought is the presence of the Lord.

The Lord, however, deals with each one according to individual capacity. Although His loved one has many lessons to learn and there are many matters she still does not understand, yet He takes account of the fact that there was some revival in her affections and so is willing to be found by her, held by her, and even to be led by her. So far as agreement and following with her vision were concerned, she had been brought through sufficient testing and experience to prove it real, and these had not been without effect.

But because she cannot yet discern what is of the spirit and what is of the soul, the Lord condescends to meet her at that level and does not attach blame to her.

"Until I had brought him into my mother's house, and into the chamber of her that conceived me." Though much of her self-life was mingled with her spiritual desires here, the Lord graciously conceded to allow some revelling because of the new intensity and vigor in her affections toward Him. He was now led by her into her mother's house and into the chamber where she had been conceived. If this "mother's house" is the system of grace, then the chamber of conception unmistakably indicates the love of God. God used the principle of grace and the heart of love to bring her forth. Thus she now seeks to hold and possess His presence in a true sense of His grace and love. In the form of a song, that is, with a heart full of praise, she leads her Lord into a secret place. Since she is a virgin maiden, there is no better place than her mother's house. This is the consciousness that she can possess Him only as a matter of grace.

This concludes another section. It brings her to revel in His presence and to hold Him with great energy, yet still in a state of imperfection. The Lord, we see, is still in a passive state in relation to her. A period of time must now elapse while she is at this stage of development in her spiritual affections.

"I charge you, O ye daughters of Jerusalem, by the roes, and by the hinds of the field, that ye stir not up, nor awake my love, till he [she] please" (3:5).

The Lord again charges those in a lesser state of grace and who are liable to interfere in His loved one's spiritual development. After this time of exercise and testing the Lord would give her a period of quietness. The implication is that He Himself is dealing with this one and no outside help is needed, therefore none are to disturb her. She has been in dead earnest in learning her lessons, and she is on the way to the accomplishment of real spiritual progress. It is the normal exercise of love to allow no interference. This maiden has learned something of what is mentioned in chapter two about the power and the fulness of resurrection life, and the life of the Cross. Though not altogether perfect,

yet she has learned these three lessons, and as a consequence
the Lord is ready to praise her.

PART THREE (3:6 - 5:1)

GROWING LOVE

THE NEW CREATION (3:6-4:6)

The previous section closed with the word that the maiden had brought her Beloved into her mother's house and into the chamber where she was conceived. The Lord evidently tarried there for quite some time, indicating that this must have been a place conducive to rest for Him. Although her holding of Him had an element which was not the best, yet this could be considered a tolerable place for Him. The implication hinted at here is that all the maiden did now stemmed from a sense of love and grace. She, for once, began to realize the vanity of self and saw that all she enjoyed came forth from God's love and that all was of His grace. Who can tell how many lessons we learn in His love and grace? How limitless and immeasurable have been the lessons taught us by the Lord Jesus Christ in the love and grace of God!

Consequently, this loved maiden, in this present state of a quiescent spirit and in the enjoyment of the Lord's presence in her mother's house and in the chamber of her conception, had come to recognize and appreciate the lessons which she needed to learn (Part Two). For God, out of His grace and love, had enabled her to gain the knowledge of what He sought in her. We all know that when one is in quest of the Lord, experiences such as described in Part Two may range from a solitary occasion to many such times. The Spirit of God does not keep a record of such experiences. Although repeated failures and repeated dealings cannot be avoided, yet all the Lord's ways with us originate from His love and grace. No matter whether it is our failure or our receiving of His dealing with us, there is always purpose within God's love and succor within His grace. We need to refrain, therefore, from concentrating on experiences. It was sufficient for this maiden that, with failures and dealings all past, she now dwelt within God's love and grace which were ever vibrant with life and ever engaged in positive activity.

In this Part (3) we immediately perceive an unprecedented progress. Both her life and her manner of living had obviously risen to a new and higher level. In this regard there are three items to note here.

The *first* is her complete union, revealed in chapter 3:6-11.

The words of this passage are not spoken by either the Beloved or His loved maiden, but rather are the words of the Holy Spirit spoken through some of the inhabitants of Jerusalem as they see a procession approaching. One of them voices a question (vs. 6), and three others reply (vss. 7-8, vss. 9-10, vs. 11), each revealing to us a part of the scene before them.

First we have the question:

"Who [or "What"] is this that cometh out of the wilderness like pillars of smoke, perfumed with myrrh and frankincense, with all powders of the merchant?" (3:6).

What is seen is a distant cloud of dust, rising like columns of smoke, approaching from the wilderness. It is actually — we learn later — caused by a procession of mighty men bearing, among other things, a litter or palanquin, and on this palanquin King Solomon and his loved maiden are riding. He is bringing her up from the wilderness, which borders on Egypt. The wilderness is a place of wandering, but now she is gradually coming forth out of that kind of life and, step by step, leaving behind her a life of wanderlust to enter into the Lord's rest. She now desires to so live that the heavenly life might be manifest and expressed through her.

The appearance of this procession is descriptive of how the loved maiden herself appears as she travels with her Beloved toward Jerusalem, the city of peace (Hebrews 7:2). And how is that? We are told, "like pillars of smoke." Smoke is something brought out and released through the action of fire, as we see in Joel 2:30, and indicates the power of the Holy Spirit investing her with new strength. Smoke is something which in itself is easily dispersed, but here that weak stuff is formed into a pillar. This implies a new steadfastness in her through being filled with the power of the Holy Spirit. Man in his natural state is very weak and unreliable, but here this maiden looks like a pillar. Grace is strong in her. The pillar speaks of dependability and established strength, as in Revelation 3:12: "Him that overcometh will I make a pillar in the temple of my God."

The mention of "myrrh" points to the sufferings and death of the Lord Jesus and to the fact that she had experienced in a subjective sense the value of those sufferings and that death. She thus bore the sweet odor and fragrance of the Cross in her life such as the Apostle Paul spoke of in Philippians 3:10. Being "perfumed" with this fragrance means that she first absorbed it in order to emit her own natural odors which were like that of smoke, the fumes of what was burnt up! It was the expulsive power of a new affection. This speaks of an inward experience which first removed from within her everything offensive, and then of being indwelt afterwards by the Spirit of God so that she could give forth the fragrance of Christ.

"Frankincense" in the text speaks of yet another sweet and fragrant spice and indicates the Lord Jesus in His risen and triumphant life, with special reference to His intercessory life of prayer as a living High Priest. It is this life of prayer of His which rises as a sweet savor unto God. The most marvelous fact is that our Lord first lived here on earth and then died, whereas in our case we must first be identified with Him in His death in order to have a release of His life through us. He lived, then died; we die (spiritually speaking), then live. Hence the myrrh is mentioned first, then the frankincense.

"With all powders of the merchant." "Merchant" is singular, and when linked with Matthew 13:45 points to the Lord Jesus. This tells us that this loved maiden not only possessed what is represented by myrrh and frankincense but also that she possessed the riches of His exalted life — all He was and had. The Lord was the merchant who had enriched her and who sold to her all of which she stood in need. A merchant does not give gratis — he sells. She therefore obtained these precious things of His grace at a price. The price she paid was an obedience and devotedness that stood every test. In exchange for that, she received of the Lord the fragrant virtues of His life. All these were complementary to the values already received from His death and resurrection.

"Behold his bed ["Behold, it is the litter"—ASV], which is Solomon's; threescore valiant men are about it, of the valiant of Israel. They all hold swords, being expert in war: every man hath his sword upon his thigh because of fear in the night" (3:7-8).

This is the first reply in answer to the question of verse 6.

The first object to come into clear view was not the palanquin upon which King Solomon was riding, but rather his couch upon which he and the loved maiden would rest in their tent at night. And what would this mean in reference to our Lord? It assuredly speaks of His triumph over all His enemies and that He has come to the place of rest. His couch is His rest of victory. But here on earth it is still nighttime with an intense darkness prevailing. Within this reign of darkness are very hostile powers which tend to challenge His rest on earth. Here, however, we see that King Solomon could still enjoy his rest in spite of the alarms and warnings of the night which came because of hostile and opposing forces. His couch, then, represents and records His victory over all the principalities and powers of darkness. He has come to the place of his rest.

"Threescore valiant men are about it . . . They all hold swords, being expert in war: every man hath his sword upon his thigh." These were mighty men of Israel, veterans in spiritual warfare. Assembling all the facts of this figurative and composite picture, it presents one outstanding thought. It is the thought that Solomon was well prepared to deal with any alarms, warnings, or assaults upon his rest which sprang from the powers of darkness. Whatever might arise, Solomon knew how to deal with it and in such a way as not to disturb his rest. In other words, no enemy attack could surprise him, and he enjoyed the rest of his victory because mighty men of spiritual strength guarded it.

The question may arise as to how his spouse fared in all the dangers of the night. The answer is, simply in Solomon's state. She and Solomon were so identified with each other at this stage that there was a perfect oneness between them. What was his, was hers. What he enjoyed, she enjoyed. This is union. It instructs us that just as this loved maiden was identified with Solomon in his perfect rest, so the saints of today may share and enjoy the rest which the Lord Jesus gained after defeating Satan and all his hosts. Today, too, there are numerous angels and faithful ones on earth who are fully prepared and ready in any emergency to defend the Lord's rest and victory by faithful affections and spiritual strength.

"King Solomon made himself a chariot of the wood of Lebanon. He made the pillars thereof of silver, the bottom thereof of gold, the covering of it of purple, the midst thereof being paved with love, for the daughters of Jerusalem" (3:9-10).

This is the second reply in answer to the one who spoke in verse 6. It mentions the next object to come into clear view, the palanquin.

Solomon's couch was what he used and enjoyed in the night. His rest in such tranquility was a demonstration to the enemy that nothing could disturb him. Now we see his "chariot." This was his means of conveyance in the daytime, and refers to his movements in fellowship with his friends.

This "chariot" is a palanquin; that is, not a chariot propelled on its own wheels but a covered litter carried by staves resting on the shoulders of living men. This reminds us of the ark of the covenant which was never to be pulled along on a cart by oxen but carried on the shoulders of the children of Kohath. The implication is clear and means that the movements of our risen Lord are borne along by those who belong to Him and who are alive with His life. This is service of a most exalted character.

The palanquin was made of cedar of Lebanon. Wood in the Scriptures is ever representative of human nature. Cedar is the superior wood and indicates our Lord's superior Manhood — tall, noble, stately, rising high in spiritual worth above ordinary men. The cedar wood points to that excellence and elevation of moral character which ever marks His movements.

The silver pillars of the palanquin speak of the grace of

redemption which is prominent wherever He moves. Objectively speaking, it is a figure of Christ brought into human history to accomplish redemption through His death; subjectively, it stresses the work of the Cross in the life of the believer, which allows no fleshly activity. That principle of the Cross renders the flesh inoperative and thus makes possible the life of Christ.

The floor of the palanquin was of gold, which means that the ground of movement was in the divine character and derived from God, so that all His movements bore the distinctive features of the divine nature. God's own holy life, of which we become partakers when we are born from above and which we obtain in that moment when we are identified with the Lord in His death, is the one foundation upon which the Lord Jesus can stand and move to the accomplishment of His purpose. Outside of God's own gift of life to us we have no status or position upon which the Lord can move.

The covering, which is better translated "seat," was of purple and sets forth the truth that the Lord is King and moves with kingly authority. He must reign. The government is upon His shoulders and therefore He sits on the throne of rule. Finally, the palanquin was curiously wrought within by the daughters of Jerusalem, and this speaks of the love of all saints for Him. Their total affections are the vehicle for His movements and goings forth.

The palanquin, therefore, with its pillars, floor, seat, and work of love, was Solomon's own chariot, but also the vehicle of movement for his spouse. Not only the chariot was her possession, but he who rode in it, even Solomon the king. And not only was the chariot a vehicle for her use in transportation, but it represented what she had become and what the king had made her through his grace.

Thus we see that the Lord finds His place of movement in the mature affections of His spouse and is borne along to His purpose by them. Such affections give full support to His every movement. How perfect, then, was the union between Solomon and this loved one. Small wonder, when the question was asked as to her well-being, that her response was to point out how it was now with Solomon. He could move to his appointed end in what she had become.

A fourth citizen of Jerusalem now speaks, giving words of exhortation:

"Go forth, O ye daughters of Zion, and behold king Solomon with the crown wherewith his mother crowned him in the day of his espousals, and in the day of the gladness of his heart" (3:11).

The "daughters of Zion" would indicate those who love and recognize responsibility for others and who have special views of the Lord's sovereignty. The crown here is neither the crown of glory nor the crown of His millennial kingdom, nor does this crown represent His power and authority to rule as the King. This is a crown of crowns which was bestowed on Solomon by his mother because of his union to this loved one.

As yet the marriage was not consummated, but this crowning was a crowning of joy in his chosen and elect one. There are two crowns spoken of in the New Testament. The one represents the glorious power of our Lord's supreme rule and authority; the other is that of joyous happiness such as the apostle mentions in I Thessalonians 2:19. The crown here, then, is the crown of joy which the Lord Jesus has in those who are espoused to Him. To Him as the King they are like a crown which gladdens His heart. From this time forth He looks upon His chosen bride as a precious crown which is His praise and glory.

"Mother" in the text has various possible meanings, such as Israel or the system of grace. But from the point of personal experience it seems more appropriate to approach it as a term referring to the human race as a whole. God is spoken of as the Father of our Lord Jesus Christ, but His human body was prepared of a human mother from the human race — one chosen out of mankind. Thus it would point in parable to the fact that the Lord has gotten out of the total human race — His mother — one who is His body and who is to be His bride — one who satisfies His heart.

It is at this point that revelation is given her that she and the King have entered into the real espousals of marriage. The supreme love and joy which stems from marriage will come after final and complete union, but Scripturally speaking we may say that such joy comes when we are experientially fully identified with the Lord in this union of affection. With the celebration of such espousals the Lord is as one crowned with joy. This concludes the comments of the four observers we have before mentioned.

Second, we note the beauty of the new creation, in chapter 4:1-5. In the record of her many and varied experiences in her previous history, the King had often encouraged her by His praise of her, as for instance in 1:15: "Behold, thou art fair, my love; behold, thou art fair." Now He unreservedly declares this to be so in view of that singular experience in chapter 3:6 in which she came to perfect union with Him. It is now certain that she will not again employ praise of Him for selfish interests, so that at this stage His praise of her can move without restraint. He, therefore, more boldly reiterates His praise:

"Behold, thou art fair, my love; behold, thou art fair" (4:1a).

There follows immediately a sevenfold description of this praise. It expresses the features of those in Christ after they have come to final and complete union with Him. There is much now that is attractive to the Lord and all is the product of His own grace and love.

The first feature is her eyes.

"Thou hast doves' eyes within thy locks" (4:1b).

This is perception. The most prominent feature in those who go on to spiritual maturity is the ability to perceive the things of the Spirit. Doves' eyes, too, are single. Doves see only one thing in their vision and for this reason and in this sense the Holy Spirit Himself is likened to a dove. He has the perfection of spiritual insight and keeps the Lord Jesus ever in view.

But there is a great peril here for believers who have this ability. The peril is in having no covering for their spiritual perceptions and, therefore, they tend to show them off before the world. The spouse, as we may now call her, has those eyes of hers "within her locks" or "behind her veil." The people of the world cannot see or understand what a believer with spiritual insight sees. They do not know there is such a faculty. Unless this spiritual ability is kept behind a covering, one can easily babble forth what one sees by spiritual perception. Such things can only be understood by spiritual persons.

Eyes which are behind a veil are not visible to the general public. Spiritual perceptions, therefore, must be hidden from the world, for the worldlings do not understand such a faculty and regard believers as having no other ability than they themselves possess. Some believers are very foolish when they express, without discrimination and often in flippant talk, the things they have received of the Spirit of God. If such are without much spiritual understanding they ought to be aware of it and confess their limited knowledge of the power and work of the Holy Spirit.

The greater measure we have of the life of the Spirit, the more dovelike vision we shall have. True spiritual perception comes from the Third Person of the Trinity. Frequently it is necessary to keep this spiritual sense veiled that it may become a beauty which the Lord Himself can enjoy and praise. How often we overlook this issue that even our eyes of spiritual understanding are for the joy and satisfaction of the Lord Jesus alone!

The second feature is her hair.

"Thy hair is as a flock of goats, that appear from mount Gilead" (4:1c).

The hair indicates special consecration and obedience, as in the case of the Nazarites (Numbers 6). In the case of Samson, who was a Nazarite, his long hair was a symbol of his consecration and was a testimony that he was wholly given up to God. Such a special consecration becomes our strength, and this strength is manifest before men, as flowing locks can so easily be seen by them. The measure, the completeness, and the purity of our consecration determines the degree and measure of our strength before men. Separation to be a holy offering unto the Lord is the fountain-head of spiritual strength.

In the Scriptures hair has yet another signification. It is the symbol of a covering. Woman's hair has identical meaning with the long hair of the Nazarite. It speaks of a position of subjection. It is necessary to bring our whole selves into subjection to the Lord and to cover up all that is of our original creation and of our natural fleshly life in order that the image and likeness of God alone may be made manifest. This subjection to the Lord is, on the part of every believer, parallel to the subjection of the woman unto the man, and the only means whereby we can show forth the authority of Christ to the world.

"As a flock of goats, that appear from mount Gilead." Goats are usually white, and when referred to in the Scriptures are chiefly used as sin offerings. One could see flocks of them on the slopes of mount Gilead where grass was very plentiful. "He shall feed . . . and his soul shall be satisfied upon . . . mount Gilead" (Jer. 50:19); "Let them feed in . . . Gilead" (Micah 7:14). This verse, therefore, refers to the spouse as being well fed and ready to be offered at any time. For where, we ask, is consecration most manifest? Is it not where souls have been in rich pasture and received much food from the hand of His grace? All the thoughts concerning hair point to a consecrated and dedicated offering of ourselves to the Lord, and in such a dedication lies the strength and obedience of the believer.

The third feature is her teeth.

"Thy teeth are like a flock of sheep that are even shorn, which came up from the washing; whereof every one bear twins, and none is barren among them" (4:2).

Teeth indicate the ability to appropriate. They are the tools with which we masticate food. Here, however, there is no reference to food itself but only a revelation of the ability to take it in. The Lord has made very plain in His Word that He has provided a sufficiency of food for our spiritual well-being. The question is our ability to appropriate His provision and use what He has provided. The ability and capacity to do so alludes not to an infant but to such mature believers as are represented by this spouse. Only a full-grown person has strong teeth for good mastication purposes.

Why the suggestion of "a flock of sheep"? Apparently it must refer to the fact that sheep graze on pasture and can distinguish what is good for them and what is not good. There is within the believer something which is of Christ, and one must be in possession of that which is derived from Him before there is this skill to discriminate what is His pasture and the food of His provision. We must possess that which is of Christ before we can receive and enjoy the things of Christ.

Wool in the Scriptures indicates carnal life and natural zeal. In Old Testament times the priests, when entering into the Holy Place, were forbidden to clothe themselves with garments of wool, but were to use linen. Fine white linen was typical of the righteousness of Christ imparted through the Holy Spirit as our natural life is removed or reckoned inoperative by the Cross. Here, then, the fact that her teeth were like a flock of shorn sheep implies that her strength and ability to appropriate spiritual provision was not a natural thing at all. When we ourselves are in search of the Lord in deeper measures, we are not to try to receive His grace or truth of His Word by natural ability, zeal, or persistence. The following of our own natural desires, irrespective of our spiritual state, will not receive the approval of the Lord. Sheep that are newly shorn and clean from washing are usually white and orderly. This shows the desire of this spouse to be thoroughly washed from all that is unsuitable so as to walk orderly in His ways.

"Every one bear twins." This gives a true picture of orderliness as we find in teeth formation, and it implies a uniform and properly progressive strength in the ability to appropriate. Twins give the idea of good and orderly ability to receive the things of the Lord. Our natural teeth come in pairs and thus we have the reference to the spouse's teeth bearing twins. This confirms the fact that the strength and ability of being able to appropriate was both uniform and orderly.

The fourth feature is her lips.

"Thy lips are like a thread of scarlet, and thy speech is comely" (4:3a).

Lips signify expression. As teeth are instruments for receiving and masticating food given by the Lord, so the lips are vehicles for expressing what has been received from Him. In the new creation the Lord not only pays attention to our spiritual perceptions, our dedication, and our food, but also to our expression. "A thread of scarlet" has two aspects of truth.

The first indicates redemption, as when Rahab bound the

scarlet thread in her window (Joshua 2:21). The other
aspect is that of authority, as in Matthew 27:28-29: "And
they stripped him, and put on him a scarlet robe. And when
they had platted a crown of thorns, they put it upon his
head, and a reed in his right hand: and they bowed the knee
before him, and mocked him, saying, Hail, King of the
Jews."

So there is, in the comely verbal expression of the spouse,
an evidence, on the one hand, that her life has been cleansed,
and, on the other, that her lips are under the authority of
her King. How different is the speech from the lips of the
heathen who reject His authority and who say, "With our
tongue will we prevail; our lips are our own: who is lord
over us?" (Psalm 12:4). Our lips need to go through the
process of redemption by submission to the authority of
Christ the King. They must not speak at random or uncon-
trolled, but must express the purity and virtue of the life of
Christ. Unless we are redeemed and brought to spiritual
maturity, then the teeth which are set within our mouth will
take in and masticate the wrong food and the speech flowing
forth from the lips will not be right.

The fifth feature is her temples.

"Thy temples are like a piece of pomegranate within thy locks"
(4:3b).

The temples indicate beauty. The word for temples may
be translated "cheeks." It is the cheeks which display beauty
and are the parts of our face which most clearly display the
emotions of joy, anger, sadness, or gladness. All such emotions are clearly exhibited to others through our facial expressions.

"Like a piece of a pomegranate within thy locks." The
reference to a piece and not to a whole pomegranate means
what has been opened and exposed. The pomegranate in
Biblical language points to fulness of life because of its many
seeds, each of which is juicy, sweet, and red. It is a delightful thing to see this beautiful appearance and fruit in the life
of a believer because of the fulness of Christ's life within.
Yet this beauty and fruitfulness is veiled from the world, for
they are within her locks or under her veil. In other words,
who can appreciate such spiritual qualities save the Lord

Himself? Although believers are in the world and a good name is much to be desired as a necessary adjunct to our testimony which is to shine before men, yet the motivation in such desire is not self-expression—not to be "before men, and to be seen of them." The only place where a believer is really on display is within the veil, behind the doors, and in the presence of the Lord. This always is the basic principle in the life of the believer.

The sixth feature is the neck.

"Thy neck is like the tower of David builded for an armoury, whereon there hang a thousand bucklers, all shields of mighty men" (4:4).

The neck represents the will of man. What a man does in his own will, and becomes proud and unrelenting in the pursuit of, is called in the Scriptures stiff-neckedness (Isaiah 3:16). The neck of the spouse represents a will in submission to the will of the Lord. To Him, such submission is a beautiful feature.

In the words of the text there is a two-fold meaning. "Thy neck is like a tower" is the first thought. This means the Lord's chosen bride is not a hunchback or one that is bent. Luke 13:11-16 tells of a woman bowed down and who could in no wise lift up herself, "whom Satan hath bound, lo, these eighteen years." This daughter of Abraham, a believer of sorts, was so bent over that she could see nothing but the earth. How different with the spouse in the text, whose neck was like a tower, which implies that she had been set free and made straight. She was no longer fettered and bound by Satan and no longer looked to the world for her satisfaction.

A neck like a tower also suggests steadfastness and upwardness of outlook. This suggests she had been established on solid spiritual ground and was no longer attracted by the world or affected by the influence of Satan.

Then we have David's name added, which suggests a second thought. "Thy neck is like the tower of David." This reference is not to any ordinary tower, but to one which was built by David. The thought is that just as this tower was David's defense in times of warfare, so also here; besides having been set free and made straight and strong, the will of this loved one had been led forward another step and brought into such complete obedience that her will had become a bulwark of defense against enemy attack. In this she was like David, the man after God's own heart, who did all God's will (Acts 13:22). How important it is, therefore, to know subjection to the Lord Jesus in order to have a will fixed in God and which is a strong tower in times of danger.

For what purpose, we may ask, was the tower built? The answer is that it was David's armory—a storehouse of weapons. In the matter of spiritual warfare the battle of life assuredly centers round the will, but in the life of the mature believer the Lord has laid up an inward strength within the will which is for the protection of the believer. In order that believers yield not again to the enemy of souls, they are made like a tower of David, who had an immovable purpose to do all the will of God. These weapons within are not for offensive use, but for defensive watchfulness. Bucklers and shields were instruments for protection under assault. The number "one thousand" of such weapons points to the sufficiency of such armory provided by the Lord so that such believers are well covered and protected. The "mighty men" show the invulnerable position secured by the Lord for His people.

We may therefore summarize: Because of her likeness to David in obedience, this spouse, in her full surrender to the Lord, was made to stand steadfast and immovable like a tower to do the will of God, and then to be alert and on her defense with a sufficiency of inward weapons against any inroad by the enemy.

The seventh feature is her breasts.

"Thy two breasts are like two young roes that are twins, which feed among the lilies" (4:5).

The breast is the seat of the emotions. This may be interpreted as two parts or sides of the chest; hence, that which makes an even balance. The most vital essence of pure emotion is our *faith* and *love* by which we embrace the Lord. Through these we are drawn closer to Him. Faith and love together constitute the one and only means through which we are united to the Lord, and thus they are like two sides of the chest of a maiden giving an even balance to the affections.

"Like two young roes." A young roe or fawn of a gazelle is timid, shy, and easily frightened, but extremely nimble. The young roes here then are emblematical of those sacred and spiritual affections which we hold and keep for the Lord. Such affections are not for the general public because of their sensitive and tender nature. They need to be guarded with care, or otherwise they lose their function.

The young fawns are referred to as twins: "two young roes that are twins." The original word would be "a pair of young deer born of the same mother." They are identical in size, implying that faith and love should grow together to identical stature. No one commended by the Lord as beautiful and fair could be great in faith and small in love. Such imbalance could not be praised as beauty. In the New Testament faith and love are set forth as of equal importance (Galatians 5:6; I Timothy 1:5, 14; Philemon 5). In the matter of spiritual reality there is no such thing as being great in love and small in faith, or great in faith and small in love. Each of these virtues may be great or small but they should be equal. Beauty of form is not to have them one-sided but to have them developed in equal proportion because they are like "two young roes that are twins."

"Which feed among the lilies." The implication here is none other than the fact that faith and love in the spouse fed and grew in an environment suitable to the nature she had received of God. "Lilies" point to such an environment and express the nurture, the holiness, and the promises of those things which are of God for the production of spiritual features. They flourish as they grow in a heavenly atmosphere and feed on pure things. Lilies speak of purity and that condition of holiness which makes the conscience free from guilt and guile. When the conscience is defiled, then there is loss in faith and love. Faith and love can grow and flourish only on the ground of a cleansed conscience. If these virtues are to develop, therefore, they must be where the Lord pastures His flock.

Third, we note the maiden's deeper search:

"Until the day break, and the shadows flee away, I will get me

to the mountain of myrrh, and to the hill of frankincense" (4:6).

Chapter 3:6-11 spoke of her union with the Lord, chapter 4:1-5 of the resultant outcome of that union, namely, that the Lord found satisfaction in His loved one and praised her beauty. Generally speaking, what followed from that union was chiefly her adoration of the King. The whole movement previous to this, recorded in chapters 1:2-2:7, has much of the maiden's praise of the King, but the King's attitude to this praise was very restrained. It is a true picture of those who, prior to deeper experiences with the Lord and deeper dealings by the Lord, love to talk incessantly about their experiences concerning spiritual status and progress and what they have obtained from the Lord through lessons learned. At the same time they will boast of their fellowship with Him—His love for them, His promises given them, and how marvellously He has answered their prayers.

Up to this time the maiden knew nothing of the third heaven nor had she been through any real dealings at the hand of the Lord. Her conversation in that immature state therefore proved her shallowness of spiritual measure; but having come through the wilderness experience we see a difference. Her speech is less voluminous; her words are fewer. Thus the words of chapter 3:6-11 are not by the spouse but by others, and those of chapter 4:1-5 are all spoken by the King.

Concerning her experience and her relationship with the King, she has now increased in spiritual capacity and calibre. We shall go no further than this at the present, but take it up later. We see that not only did she talk less, but she was more attentive at listening. In truth, it is the believer who does not talk much who listens best. Having passed through the experience of the Cross this maiden was under far more perfect control by the Holy Spirit, and all her feelings were better regulated. She could now remain in quietness of spirit at the Lord's praise of her, without private self-exaltation and the elation of those natural energies which produce pride.

On the contrary, she had a more active sense of her own weakness and freely admitted that the deeper work of the Cross was indispensable to her progress. We see, therefore, that after the description of her experience by the others, she herself did not reiterate anything of that experience. And after the King had praised her well, there was none of the former pride in using words to talk about her own goodness. She had a very short word to say, and that in a very subdued spirit. Thus spiritual features were developing in her.

"I will get me to the mountains of myrrh, and to the hill of frankincense." From this brief remark of hers, we observe that the maiden fully realized her present limited state of attainment and that spiritual features needed still more development. The future is taken up in these words: "Until the day break, and the shadows flee away." They point to a realization in her that she had yet to come to the climax of spiritual maturity and that, since there were shadows in the present, she was awaiting with anticipation that fuller and brighter day.

The words also reveal this other facet of her humble attitude, namely, that she was very much alive to this need in her spiritual condition, even after receiving such assured praise and commendation from the Lord as we have seen in former verses. Could it be, she probably thought, that her union with the Lord was not vital and real enough? Could it be that spiritual features in her were not pleasing enough for His satisfaction? The Holy Spirit's favorable view of her state and the laudatory praises of the Lord Jesus are to show us that in the sight of God she had reached a point of height and depth. There was no barrier between her and Him, and the Lord appeared satisfied with her present state and found no lack in her.

Nevertheless, this was but one side of the picture. It was, as it were, the Lord's satisfaction with this present stage of growth. Any person of advanced experience would realize that a fully mature and perfected believer should be free from shadows of any description and be flooded with the morning light in the Lord.

But this maiden was conscious that within her life there still lingered certain shadows, and that the perfect day had not yet dawned. The more one abides in the light, the more one recognizes darkness. The more perfect one is, the more conscious one becomes of imperfections. So likewise, the more mature a believer becomes, the more he will feel his immaturity. The more a believer walks in the light, the greater seems to be the need for the cleansing blood of Christ. The more he receives praise of the Lord, the more he feels the sky of spiritual life has not yet come into fullest glow. Thus the maiden came to feel that in a measure, as formerly, she was still wandering in somewhat of a wilderness.

What then was to be done? Before such a perfect light could dawn and all shadows flee away, she felt she must go to the mountains of myrrh and to the hill of frankincense and abide there until the day did break and the shadows flee away. But one is always reluctant to leave the present ground of attainment and reach out further for still higher things.

In the experience of the believer, the final state of perfection must await the Lord's return. The only solution for present deliverance is on the mountain of myrrh and the hill of frankincense. The implication is that — in spite of the Lord's commendation and praise, and even though the Holy Spirit recognizes this union with Christ in spiritual affections —the maiden was still conscious of remaining weakness, corruption, guile, and inability to reach the fullest measure of spiritual affections. Prior to, and in anticipation of a realization of a state of perfection, she must therefore still walk in the way of the Cross and continue to claim the Lord as her life for the future. She was, as it were, thinking aloud something like this:

"When I began to leave the wilderness world behind me, myrrh and frankincense were the fragrance of my life. Thus I need to hasten now to the mountain of myrrh and hill of frankincense and literally steep myself in these rich odors. Was it not these sweet odors which brought about a deeper union between the Lord and me and which brought forth His satisfaction and praise of me?

"I must, therefore, live on the mountain of myrrh and hill of frankincense. If, through the means of deeper fellowship in His sufferings and death, a greater deliverance from the wilderness world can be attained, then the Cross and I must know a deeper union. In the endurance of yet greater afflictions, and in my going down to a deeper death in Christ, I must move forward to the perfect break of day. And if, by trusting more fully and committing myself more completely, I may live by His life and move step by step to higher ground, then I am willing to renounce all my old life and yield myself so completely to Him that He will find nothing of the old creation.

"In comparing my former experience with what I now desire to move into, myrrh and frankincense were then only as drops of perfume. Henceforth these sweet odors must be like mountains and hills in their fulness so that, by this fuller identification with Christ in His Cross and resurrection, there may spring up within me a transcendent overcoming power, a greater degree of spiritual perception, a closer relationship between my soul and God, and a more complete deliverance from this wilderness world."

THE CALL TO THE HEAVENLIES (4:7-15)

The first thing is the call (vs. 7-8), and here (as is agreed by most Bible expositors) it is the King who speaks concerning upward spiritual movement. After the maiden had taken this further step in deeper comprehension of the Cross and resurrection, the King could now address her thus:

"Thou art all fair, my love; there is no spot in thee." (4:7).

Prior to this the King had only said, "Thou art fair" (4:1), but now He says, "Thou art *all* fair."

In other words, He is now saying that she is altogether lovely because all her blemishes had been removed by the further application of the Cross. Through the processes of discipline these blemishes had been removed as unsuitable for a bride. At the present time nothing remained in her but the holy and heavenly life of her Lord since she had taken up her full portion of blessing and was standing on new territory in His resurrection life. We can see her now as being one who is altogether lovely—"There is no spot in thee." Thus the Lord delights to view those who have come so far and made such response.

"Come with me from Lebanon, my spouse, with me from Lebanon: look from the top of Amana, from the top of Shenir and Hermon, from the lions' dens, from the mountains of the leopards" (4:8).

In Part Two of the Song the King had demanded two things of His chosen loved one. First, He would have her rise up out of her circumstance and second, go along with Him in His circumstance. In His dealing with her at that period we saw that she rose up but did not learn how to go along with Him into His circumstances of leaping upon the mountains and skipping upon the hills. The demand of the Lord, therefore, was held in abeyance.

But the Lord never lowers His standard nor surrenders His purpose for His chosen ones. He bides His time and waits until developing maturity prepares us for the fuller response demanded. But He never changes His call unto His full purpose. Often after His dealings with us we come to a fulness of time, and at this more developed stage He will call again unto His full purpose as before. "Come away with me." There is urgency now—a pressing of the call, since He twice repeats it: "Come with me . . . with me."

The Lord is now calling her to heavenly elevation. Some scholars suppose that the words "from Lebanon" denote a call to *depart* from Lebanon. Personally, I feel the contrary. "From" does not necessarily imply a departure; but here, very obviously, it is part of a poetic composition and form of words. He is asking her to come to several high lookouts from which she can take in the view "from Lebanon." It is not a matter of her *departure* from Lebanon; but, on the contrary, we see her coming with Him into a spiritual outlook represented by what is in the fragrant heights of Lebanon. The picture of the glorious pinnacles of Lebanon indicates a new phase in her experience.

Lebanon very plainly points toward a new and elevated position where the scented cedar wood is generally the most outstanding feature. The cedar is a tall, noble, scented wood. The high mountains of Scripture indicate our leaving the earth level to move up to a heavenly position—being in the world but jutting far out of it into the heavenlies. The call which comes to the maiden here is one of ascent into heavenly elevation. To put it in a more specific and certain way, it is precisely a call to the believer to be with Christ in His exaltation and to look downward to earthly levels from that elevated position of favor and authority.

The believer's position should be on the mountaintop. There are many who have failed and fallen down precipices, but their original and intended position in Christ is one of heavenly elevation. In Him the heavenly state is ever present and, indeed, one is actually surrounded by, and conscious of, all heavenly things, and thus is correspondingly far above the levels of earth. Thus, we find that there are mountaintops in our experience, and that there is, as we shall see, more than one mountain we may enjoy. Since one is far above the limitations and enclosures which often bind us while on lower levels, these three peaks of Lebanon give the idea of enlargement.

"Amana" means "confirmation" or "truth." (It is a word related to "amen" — "so be it.") We may often look down from this vantage ground and view things from the heights of divine thoughts, gazing upon an all-inclusive Christ in reality and truth.

"Shenir" indicates a flexible armor. It apparently has reference to the whole armor given by the Holy Spirit. It focuses our thoughts on possible warfare and the need for full equipment. The equipment is found in spiritual elevation, where there is perception which floods all with heavenly light and with which we can view the movements of the enemy beneath.

"Hermon" denotes destruction and undoubtedly speaks of the victory of the Cross and how the Lord Jesus, as the eternal Son of God, was manifested to destroy the works of the devil. The believer views Christ's full victory only by conscious association with Him in His exaltation over all which belongs to the earth sphere.

There are many high places in this matter of spiritual elevation. These high places speak of spaciousness, where there is room for enlargement and development. However in Ephesians, chapters one and two, we are led to see that the sphere of the heavenlies is precisely where the presence of the enemy is very real and operative (Eph. 6:12).

"The lions' dens . . . the mountains of the leopards." Walking on the **mountain tops** of Lebanon and looking out from its high points of Amana, Shenir, and Hermon, one could not help but encounter at the same time the lions' dens and the mountains of the leopards. This was a region where lions roared on earth and where leopards devoured their prey. But the lions' dens and the mountains of the leopards' habitat were in the very regions which represented the heavenlies.

That which we are confronted with prior to our knowing the experience of spiritual elevation into the realm of the heavenlies is no more than the works of the enemy upon earth. After the further experience of entrance into the reality of the heavenly places, however, we are brought to (and should desire to be) where the enemy has his hide-out, in order that we may not only witness the works of the enemy but come to grips with him face to face. Concerning lions, the Scripture calls attention to their roaring. The enemy's work is to frighten and terrify. As to leopards, the Book of books focuses attention on their appetites. This aspect of the enemy's work is to devour.

In calling His loved one to a position of spiritual elevation, the Lord did not say that from this time forth everything would be bright and beautiful. He shows her that though this mountain-top life was to be her sphere of movement, yet nevertheless it was a realm where lions and leopards, representative of malignant powers, were close at hand. If one does not know the experience of the heavenlies as in Ephesians, chapters one and two, then he can never understand the spiritual warfare of Ephesians, chapter six. A spiritually elevated man knows how real and near is the presence of the enemy. Since there is this fact of circumstance, the Lord invites us to look down from a high position. Our mountaintop is the height of divine truth. Our mountaintop is protective armor. Our mountaintop is the Lord's triumph over all the powers of destruction. Concerning heavenly things, one must stand on heavenly ground to discern clearly the issues of a heavenly character. Yea, even in the matter of issues of a purely earthly nature one cannot discern their real substance with any clarity unless the issues are viewed from the heavenly point of view. Heavenly ground is the one and only place which affords a proper vantage-point view of things.

Not infrequently, we presumptuously endeavor to solve

problems and difficulties by means of earthly or natural perception, and this invariably brings frustration and confusion.
Even in dealing with some minor issues of life we need to
view them from heavenly ground, otherwise we shall miss
the mark entirely in finding a solution. Yet we must be
fully aware of the fact that in this elevated region we are in
close proximity to those malignant powers which are represented by "the lions' dens" and "the mountains of leopards."

To summarize this matter: Whatever we see and observe
in the heights of divine love, we must never forget that there
is an ever-present enemy. Therefore, when we have seen
things from a heavenly viewpoint, we must ever recall that
we came to this in spite of lions and leopards. Those who
have known mountain-top experience and vision know how
stealthily the enemy prowls around such persons of spiritual
perception. Those, then, who have viewed matters from the
heights of God's Land of Promise must, at the same time,
keep in vision the utter defeat of the enemy.

In the matter of spiritual warfare, there is first of all a
position to be taken; and second, there is vision to be
granted. Without that position it is impossible to perceive
the true character of the enemy's personality. Without this
heavenly vision, on the other hand, it is impossible to see
the subtlety of his movements. These are two prerequisites
without which it is impossible to fight or even to engage the
enemy in any type of warfare at all.

This indeed was an unprecedented call to His loved one.
It was a great and demanding call. For a weak and delicate
maiden who, by nature, would find it an almost insurmount-
able difficulty to climb such mountains and gain such lofty
heights, it was a tremendous challenge—to say nothing of
entering into a region where there were lions' dens and
leopards' hide-outs! But now, having heard this call to
spiritual elevation, what is her response?

In this place, we have a speechless but real response. She
moves at His call but does not speak, and this brings forth
this word from the King:

**"Thou hast ravished my heart, my sister, my spouse; thou hast
ravished my heart with one of thine eyes, with one chain of thy
neck" (4:9).**

For the first time the King addresses her as "my sister, my spouse." Here her desires for Him are identified with His desires for her. Here the King looks upon her as one in whom He could confide and to whom He could now share everything. Her affections have gone beyond the ordinary at this stage and, being thus mature and pure, are capable of entering into conjugal relationship.

Essentially, this loved one had endured and experienced numberless disciplinary dealings until at present there is manifested in her body all the spiritual features of a new creation. It was this which gave so much pleasure and satisfaction to the King's heart. You see, then, that the King loved her so because her chief attraction was that she had been responsive and subject to the unconditional work of the Holy Spirit and had emerged altogether lovely. Thus she ravishes His heart.

Here, for the first time, the King addresses His loved one as "sister" and this because they were of kindred nature. "For both he that sanctifieth and they who are sanctified are all of one" (Hebrews 2:11). Abraham's wife Sarah was his sister of sorts. Isaac, too, was married to one of his own kin. Jacob married into his mother's brother's family, whereas it was quite otherwise with profane Esau who took a heathen wife. So also with the Lord Jesus, who gives Himself and His love to that one company of people who, being born of the Father in heaven, possess the same essential life as Himself.

"Thou hast ravished my heart." That is: "You have seized upon My love and drawn Me to yourself. You have caused Me to transport with joy and to find My satisfaction in being close to you. You have challenged Me to go along with you, since you have so responded to My desires. Moreover, your eyes have proved more eloquent than words spoken by the lips, so that by your mere glance I know now that you are willing to go along the whole way with Me."

"Thou hast ravished my heart with one of thine eyes"— with a look of spiritual perception. The message in the eye can be very eloquent. Did not our Lord Himself once look upon Peter and melt his heart with one glance from His eye? A stranger cannot read and understand the glance of a lover's eye, but the loved one can interpret in it most clearly the heart's desire of the lover. "With one chain of thy neck." Not only did her eye speak to Him but He noticed the affirmative response of her neck. The chain on the neck was representative of obedience to divine precepts as in Proverbs 1:9: "For they shall be an ornament of grace unto thy head, and chains about thy neck." He was thus saying to her in effect: "By your obedience to the teaching and instruction of the Holy Spirit, which has produced features of spiritual wisdom in your character, you have ravished My heart with love for you. Thus encouraged, I know you will allow Me to lead you forward and onward."

The next thing is the inner relationship (4:10-15).

"How fair is thy love, my sister, my spouse! how much better is thy love than wine! and the smell of thine ointments than all spices!" (4:10).

It is as though He had never before so praised her love. God the Father has chosen to draw man to Himself by means of His Son, Jesus Christ. In order to accomplish this the Lord God placed His beloved Son in this world so that man could be invited to love Him and thus again express God's love here on earth. When man is drawn thus to Christ, as is this maiden, it is in reality a response to God's invitation to love Him. The love which finds expression here is the response of man's affection to God through the Lord Jesus Christ and is really a heart-felt "Thank You" to God for His love. Christ is the center to which all response to the love of God moves.

Such love to Christ can be offered by a believer only as the result of constant dealings through discipline. Such a love is thus perfected and matured as time moves on until such a believer finds that his heart's affections are no longer set upon the things of the world but are wholly set upon the things which are above in heaven. It is when a believer comes to this state that the Lord bursts forth in gladsome praise: "How fair is thy love . . . how *much better* is thy love than wine!"

In chapter 1:2 when the maiden praised the King for His love, she merely declared His love to be *"better* than wine." From a comparison with the present words of the King we gain the knowledge that a believer's appreciation of the love of Christ is far less than His expressed love for him. Although we feel His love to be exceedingly precious, yet we little comprehend how precious that love really is. We know well the story of the love of David and Jonathan and how "they kissed one another, and wept one with another, until David exceeded" (I Samuel 20:41). Our Lord, then, of whom David was a type, is thus pre-eminent, and the expression of His love far exceeds ours for Him.

"The smell of thine ointments than all spices." The loved maiden now bears upon her person the fragrance of the King's ointments. The King had been anointed with the Holy Spirit and the maiden had now received the same anointing by the same Spirit. It was the oil which ran down from Aaron's beard and went down to the skirts of his garment (Psalm 133:2).

Our attention is directed here, however, not to the ointment itself but rather to the fragrance of its sweet scent, which sets forth the rich and varied features of that anointing. Fragrance is something invisible and it cannot be discerned save by the sense of smell. Fragrance is the world's most inexplicable commodity. Have you not had the experience of sensing a certain spiritual quality about a believer who seemed to exude a special spiritual influence over you and for which you could not find words to describe? That is fragrance! It is the fruit of a life obedient to the Holy Spirit, and such a fragrance far surpasses all the virtues which the world can muster together. Not infrequently we have to admit that a non-believer may excel such-and-such a believer on account of some special natural endowment, but this can never be compared with the fragrance which comes forth from a life fashioned by the Spirit of God.

The "smell" here differs from aforementioned scents. Of all the scents in the world and of all spices of the natural life, none could equal the fragrant anointings now upon this maiden. It was this anointing which now enabled her lips to drop honey as the honeycomb.

"Thy lips, O my spouse, drop as the honeycomb" (4:11a).

Honey, however, cannot be made in a brief period of time. It requires a great deal of work over a period of time to manufacture and accumulate honey. And this is the pre-requisite for one who would be instructed continuously in the presence of the Lord. It is diligent work and patient gathering. Out of the mouth of this maiden, therefore, came no idle words, jesting, or untrue, disparaging words, but only those words which were sweet and edifying. Her words were not impulsive like the babbling of a mountain stream on its way out, but rather like the gentle dripping of the honey-comb—drop by drop.

When some people talk—and they simply must talk—their speech is like a rapid stream of water, even though their theme may be of spiritual content. The manner of speaking, however, displays the lack of any inner strength of grace. The emphasis here on the manner of speech from the King's spouse was not only on how slowly the honey distilled from her lips but also on what was hidden and resident within her.

It is therefore said of her:

"Honey and milk are under thy tongue" (4:11b).

You can see from this that there was an inner storage of abundant good. Honey represents that which strengthens weakness, and milk is for the building up of what is young and tender. And so bountiful and plentiful was her store that she was ever ready and fully prepared to distribute to those in need. Nevertheless, this distribution was not with outward show of what she had stored within. Many tend to show off what they have, but the store of honey and milk of this mature spouse was under her tongue and not manifest as it would have been had it been seen upon her lips.

"The smell of thy garments is like the smell of Lebanon" (4:11c).

Garments in Scripture speak of all that has to do with out-ward attitudes, such as behavior, actions, social pleasures, good manners, and all which has external appearance, just as clothes are the visible covering for the body and easily noticed by others. Her natural habitat now was Lebanon's mount. She would still have to walk on earth, but her gar-ments of external behavior all carried the fragrance of that spiritual elevation represented by Lebanon. The fact that she did, in reality, company with the Lord in regions ele-vated far above the world meant that unconsciously she was shedding forth the fragrance of this transcendent and lofty position.

"A garden inclosed is my sister, my spouse; a spring shut up, a fountain sealed" (4:12).

You will notice there is mention of "a garden" in this verse 12; "an orchard" in verse 13; and "my garden" and "his garden" in verse 16; and also of "my garden" in 5:1. All these are in the singular. Then there is mention of "gardens" and "waters" and "streams" in 4:15, all of which are in the plural. The thought of a garden was God's original thought, as is seen in the beginning of the Scriptures.

Thus, after creation of the universe and of man, God planted a garden. A garden is neither common ground nor ground for the planting of things at random, nor is it ground for mere agricultural purposes, but for the production of something for beauty and pleasure. In a garden there may be trees; but the thought is not for timber. There may be fruit, but the value is not calculated in terms of commercial produce. The one and only objective is flower and blossom, which are to be gathered as something beautiful and exotic.

In this figurative language, therefore, we see that this maiden has now come to a spiritual position where she was of delight and satisfaction to the Lord. She had come to the realization, too, that, after all, she did not exist for herself alone, but that she was for the pleasure and satisfaction of her Bridegroom Lover. In this imagery lay the thought of a very high calling. She was not a garden merely but "a garden inclosed," which included "a spring shut up, a fountain sealed." This implies that she was exclusively for the Bridegroom-Elect's pleasure. A garden indeed, but she was not a public garden.

Thus all the beauty of spiritual feature and heavenly comeliness of her person was for no other person's delight than her one and only Lover. Numbers 19:15 tells us that "every open vessel, which hath no covering bound upon it, is unclean." An open vessel is for public usage and, being open, is exposed to every kind of disease and adverse influence. What is not wholly set aside for the Lord Jesus alone is open to imbibe anything. If only believers today would be inclosed more than they are, and if only their coverings were a little more close-fitting, the Lord's work would be much easier. Also in these words there is the thought implied of keeping oneself chaste and pure. An inclosed garden is clean ground, and cleansing is synonymous with being set aside for the Lord's own usage. Whether there be in our garden a well or a spring, these, too, are not for public usage nor are their waters to run at random into every outside place.

"Thy plants are an orchard of pomegranates, with pleasant fruits; camphire, with spikenard, spikenard and saffron; calamus and cinnamon, with all trees of frankincense; myrrh and aloes, with all the chief spices" (4:13-14).

The word "plants" in the Hebrew text means "sprouts" or "shoots." In addressing His loved one thus, the Lord is pointing out that she is now full of power — the power which conquers death and rises above it in resurrection life, as evidenced in Aaron's budded rod.

This vitality of life is likened unto an orchard of pomegranates. The meaning inherent in the pomegranate is abundance of fruit. It is full of edible and sweet seed. This loved maiden of His was not only full of the power of resurrection life but also bore the fruits of such a life. Moreover, as mentioned in a previous portion, her cheeks were likened unto the pomegranate which is not only renowned for fruit but distinguished for beauty. This orchard of pomegranates was both a garden most beautiful, and full of the choicest of fruits. It was a garden rich with every choice and varied kind of fruit.

The numerous plants and trees mentioned in these verses have either an emphasis upon the color or upon the fragrance. Everything of beauty and fragrance lies in spiritual maturity. Toward the end of verse 14 mention is made of "all trees of frankincense" and "all chief spices." This shows how a believer can become fully pleasing to the Lord.

These fruits of grace are not single only but of several kinds and of great variety. Nothing is lacking. "And God is able to make all grace abound toward you; that ye, always having all sufficiency in all things, may abound to every good work" (II Corinthians 9:8) ; "For this cause we also, since the day we heard it, do not cease to pray for you, and to desire that ye might be filled with the knowledge of his will in all wisdom and spiritual understanding; that ye might walk worthy of the Lord unto all pleasing, being fruitful in every good work, and increasing in the knowledge of God; strengthened with all might, according to his glorious power, unto all patience and longsuffering with joyfulness" (Colossians 1:9-11). The fruits spoken of in the first section indicate the fruit of the Spirit in the life of the believer, whereas the fragrance of everything in the second section denotes the blessings and graces of the Holy Spirit.

"A fountain of gardens, a well of living waters, and streams from Lebanon" (4:15).

The fountain and the well with the flowing streams were for irrigating the garden, thus providing the means of growth for the lawn, the flowers, and the trees. A well is a storage or a depository for living water, while a fountain bubbles forth to flow with streams. In John 4:11 we are told that "the well is deep," which points to a capacity to hold and store up the inflow of hidden springs, while the fountain has a continuous outflow. A well speaks of depth, and a fountain tells of energetic and continuous outflow.

This garden of the King had both a well and a fountain which provided life-giving energy and outflow to all the plants. In the garden of Eden we read of a river which divided into four heads and which thus watered all the garden. In the New Jerusalem we also see a river of life — "a pure river of water of life, clear as crystal, proceeding out of the throne of God and of the Lamb" (Revelation 22:1). The New Jerusalem is a garden city. The river of life with its continual refreshing describes the work and function of the Holy Spirit in the lives of the saints. It was this flow of living waters which caused Solomon's garden to bring forth the finest fruits and the most exquisite beauty. The waters did not originate in the garden but flowed down from the heights of Lebanon.

If the Lord Jesus had not ascended into heaven there could have been no release of the life of the Spirit. Thus He said, "It is expedient for you that I go away: for if I go not away, the Comforter will not come unto you; but if I depart, I will send him unto you" (John 16:7). All the spiritual refreshment and irrigation which flows into the lives of believers today is the outflow of the Spirit of life from the Lord's presence as He represents us before the Father in heaven.

THE LIFE OF LOVE (4:16-5:1)

"Awake, O north wind; and come, thou south; blow upon my garden, that the spices thereof may flow out. Let my beloved come into his garden, and eat his pleasant fruits" (4:16).

The previous portions dealt with the beauty of the new-creation work (4:1-5); the full and deep resolve in the maiden (4:6); her elevated position with Christ in the heavenlies (4:7-15). All this was the King's declaration of His own satisfaction in His loved one. It was the King speaking of the reasons why this relationship between Him and His loved one was so satisfying.

First, there is the response of the bride.

There are two aspects in her response. "Awake, O north wind" — and how chilling, frosty, and penetrating that can be! "Come, thou south" — and how mild, gentle, and pleasurable that can be! The spouse realizes that in her relation to the King she was as a garden in which were many spiritual fruits and blessings of grace. Now, no matter whether her circumstances are favorable or not, she will not be adversely influenced by them, but rather she will use them to draw fragrance from herself and waft it abroad in season and out of season. She had arrived at a state of grace wherein she recognized that the crux of spiritual prosperity hinged upon the inner man of the heart and not upon external circumstances. If there is fruit and fragrance within, then it matters not whether the north wind or south wind blows. These would only waft her inner fragrance farther afield.

This maiden was no longer bound within the walls of one fixed set of circumstances, but could live and flourish in any exterior condition. She was confidently aware of the fact that if there were fulness of spiritual grace within, then there would be no difficulty in adjusting to any circumstance which might arise. In this she was certainly one with the Apostle Paul in his testimony in Philippians 4:12: "I know both how to be abased, and I know how to abound: every where and in all things I am instructed both to be full and to be hungry, both to abound and to suffer need"; also in 1:20: "So now also Christ shall be magnified in my body, whether it be by life, or by death."

Her cry in this verse, which is an evidence of her flourishing spiritual condition, is also evidence of her faith. The south wind and the north wind are representative of different circumstances appointed by the sovereign choice of the Holy Spirit to develop the fragrance of her garden, and she acknowledged the right of the Spirit of God in His choice of such. Although pleasant was the south wind and fearful the north wind, yet for one whose abode was in the heavenlies, both winds were of equal value. She had the blessed assurance that in every place and in all things, since circumstances are engineered and controlled by the Holy Spirit, these would release the spiritual grace stored up within. In this she was, in a special way, looking to the Holy Spirit to accomplish and perfect His work and purpose through every circumstance.

Aside from these representations or communications from the Holy Spirit, the spouse gradually became less vocal. Her attitude was that, inasmuch as there had been planted within her many and varied fragrant plants, and that the Holy Spirit would use winds of circumstance to waft abroad the outflowing spices, and that the Lord had planted her to be His garden and bestowed grace so that she could bear pleasant fruit; then she ought to allow Him access within her garden to come, gather, and enjoy the fruits therein. Her first remark described herself as "my garden" — then almost immediately she changed the expression to "His garden" — "His own garden." In other words, my garden is His garden. The whole garden of her inner life was for Him and so were all its fruits. Thus we see that the very fruits of the Spirit which adorn the lives of the saints, far from being the boast of the believer who bears them, are for the sole pleasure of the Lord and for the sole glory of God. Here this loved maiden is unconditionally rededicating herself wholly to the Lord and to whatever He purposes to do here on earth.

Second, there is the reply of the Lord.

"I am come into my garden, my sister, my spouse: I have gathered my myrrh with my spice; I have eaten my honeycomb

with my honey; I have drunk my wine with my milk: eat, O
friends; drink, yea, drink abundantly, O beloved" (5:1).

This was the Lord's garden. From this statement we learn
that He had not always frequented it, but had come only
in response to special entreaty. Let us remember this solemn
lesson, that though a first dedication may make us truly the
Lord's, yet only many and constant dedications can ever
persuade the Lord to come into His garden in this manner.
He will come only when there are fruit and spice to satisfy.
Let us take heed lest self-satisfaction beset our souls in sup-
posing that all is well enough simply because we belong to
the Lord. Many, many times this fact ought to come to us
as a repeated warning, and again and again we should intreat
the Lord to come to us and find what He wants. Or else,
in a moment all unawares, you may discover that the Lord
has not really come into His garden at all.

Every dedication offered to the Lord is accepted by Him.
Each time this maiden entreated Him, the Lord responded.
That made up her spiritual history. If I am not mistaken
in saying so, this, perhaps, is the kind of prayer which most
easily gains an answer. The Lord was able to receive all as
His own. Eight different times He mentions the possessive
"my" — my sister, my spouse, my myrrh, my spice, my honeycomb, my honey, my wine, my milk! He receives all which
is offered to Him as the fruit of the Spirit but never the wages
of wickedness nor the earnings of a harlot. "Thou shalt not
bring the hire of a whore, or the price of a dog, into the
house of the LORD thy God for any vow: for even both these
are abomination unto the LORD thy God" (Deut. 23:18).
Nothing is implied in this loved maiden's life but that all
she had to offer was a matter of sheer delight to Him.

At this point the Lord has taken a position in relation to
His loved one which He did not have in the first section of
the Song. In this present state then, by what He had truly
found in her and received from her, He could see the fruit
of His travail.

We must pay strict attention to the fact that this advanced
dedication and this kind of reception are very different from
any ordinary dedication on our part and from any ordinary
receiving of us by the Lord. The former and early dedication

of ourselves to Him is one of committal into the hands of
the Lord to allow Him to have His way with us. The present
thought is concerned with a dedication which results from
His full work within us. It is not receiving anything from
the Lord's hand but, rather, offering to Him a life filled full
with His own work and labor of love. Therefore this fulness,
this delight, this fruitfulness, this glory, should all be given
to the Lord. What we have here is the dedication of all the
sweet spices and fruits of the garden unto the Lord.

In the same way the reception by the Lord is after the
same style. His former acceptance of what the maiden had
to offer pertained only to an opportunity for Him to cultivate, till, and plant the ground of her heart and thus do His
work within her. The acceptance of her offering here has
nothing more to do with opportunity to plant but, rather,
to give Him the opportunity to enjoy all which has grown
up within her. In the beginning, believers are like a piece
of uncultivated ground which has been dedicated to the
Lord, allowing Him to begin the transforming work of
making it into a beautiful garden. The question at hand
is: For whom is the garden? The experienced believer knows
that the latter and more complete dedication is a much more
difficult one than the former one, and much more glorious.
It is only that which can come through much labor of the
Lord in us. But it is this kind of dedication which means
that the Lord can gather the fruit of His travail.

"Eat, O friends; drink, yea, drink abundantly, O beloved."
Who, after all, is meant by these friends and beloved? The
Lord was now enjoying His loved one as a fragrant garden
in His own right as her Saviour and Lord. It would appear,
therefore, that these friends and beloved would indicate that
the Three Persons — the whole Trinity — One God — are
here together in the receiving of, and in the enjoyment of,
all the good of this garden of spiritual fruit now matured
in this loved one. It is God alone, and not man, who receives
the fruit of a believer's life.

PART FOUR (5:2 - 7:13)

TRANSFORMING LOVE

THE FURTHER CHALLENGE OF THE CROSS
(5:2-6:3)

The *first* matter is the call.

"I sleep, but my heart waketh: it is the voice of my beloved that knocketh, saying, Open to me, my sister, my love, my dove, my undefiled: for my head is filled with dew, and my locks with the drops of the night" (5:2).

At this point her former manner of profitless service and her life in the flesh had come to a standstill. She was as one in rest. No movement, no activity, no scheming, no wrestling, no self-assertion, and no anxiety arising from the flesh asserting itself. The experience of the Cross had dealt with her sins and with all that was derived from fleshly energy. Carnal life had subsided, and she was in sweet spiritual repose. We can see, then, that sin was non-active and the natural self was inoperative. Her whole being had been brought to a seeming state of love-repose in the Beloved.

While this was so on one hand, yet, on the other, she was not without a certain form of activity. There was an inner activity of meditation, of faith, of claim, of life, of work; for within her was a vibrant flow of life — the resurrection life of Christ whose wondrous life was present and living within her through the indwelling presence of the Holy Spirit. The outward expression was one of quiet rest and sweet calm of soul, but the inner spirit was alive and active.

Here there is seen the very great difference between the outer and inner man of the believer. One should be at rest outwardly but very much awake and alert inwardly and not at all sleepy. This picture coincides precisely with the Apostle Paul's testimony in Galatians 2:20: "I am crucified with Christ: nevertheless I live; yet not I, but Christ liveth in me." In this the apostle personified a complete union and communion with the Lord Jesus Christ, and such a person is unusually sensitive, alert, and full of feeling to any still small voice of the Lord's speaking. This inner man never slumbers. As soon as the Lord called she immediately heard Him and recognized that He was speaking to her in the most affectionate terms — "my love, my dove, my undefiled."

For what purpose did the Lord now call? We read that He knocked on her door, pleading, "Open to me, my sister." In the early part of the Song the Lord made Himself known to her as King and sought for a throne of authority in the heart of His loved one. Then He came to her with a further call, desiring to deliver her from the confines of a self-erected wall so that she might enjoy Him in resurrection life in all His arranged circumstances. Finally, having revealed Himself as her Bridegroom-Elect, He developed the love relationship between them.

In this verse there is a totally different kind of revelation of Himself to her. "My head is filled with dew, and my locks with the drops of the night." What sort of picture is this? What does it signify? Apparently He is speaking of Himself and portraying His agony in the Garden of Gethsemane. In that garden His blessed head was filled with the night dew as He wrestled in prayer, while the drops of the night fell upon Him. "And being in an agony he prayed more earnestly: and his sweat was as it were great drops of blood falling down to the ground" (Luke 22:44). Thus, unmistakenly, He made known to His own that He was "a man of sorrows, and acquainted with grief" (Isaiah 53:3).

In the former portions we have seen the Cross in its first effect which was for the remission of sins. Then we saw the Cross uniting the believer to Christ in the most intimate love union and relationship. Still later we saw the effect of the Cross in delivering the believer from the appeal of the world and the corruption of self. All these things we have seen exhibited in this loved maiden, and we have witnessed her progressive victory as well as a developing understanding of the values of the Cross. Following such tremendous exercises and such spiritual attainment one might well imagine that they are the sum total of all spiritual experience, and that nothing remains but a few steps to physical resurrection and eternal glory.

But not so! There is yet another deep phase of the Cross in its application to the believer — a phase with which even this loved maiden was as yet unfamiliar and uncomprehending. It was an aspect of the Cross to which she might have claimed a little experience, but which at the most was extremely superficial and elementary. She already knew, indeed, that there is a peculiar suffering attached to the Cross in human experience, but she was unaware as to the scope of that suffering in its real depth and breadth. She was quite aware and very much exercised in the application of the Cross to her inward life, but she did not know, as yet, the extent to which that Cross would shape and mold her whole being. The Lord is now calling her, therefore, as a believer-disciple, into an experience of the full mystery of the Cross.

The awful truth of which Gethsemane spoke so eloquently was that God the Father became the despiser of His beloved Son with that despite which is spoken of in Isaiah 53:3b-4: "He was despised . . . we did esteem him stricken, smitten of God, and afflicted." Though an ordinary believer may be aware of the redemptive aspect of the sacrifice of the Cross, yet it is possible not to know in experience this shame of being despised by the Father. It was this phase which caused the greatest suffering to the Lord Jesus Christ.

Among His many former afflictions it was possible for Him to find a glorious aspect to such trials and to be upheld and comforted in them, for in all such former afflictions the Father's presence was with Him. But now — on this awful day — He was not only despised by men but seemingly so by the Father, too. The Father turned His face away, and not only that — what befell Him at the Cross appeared to be the smitings of God. One could see in them, as it were, the very hand of God. The punishment of God was so manifest in this great substitutionary sacrifice that He was utterly despised by men, and it was this mingling of divine and human despite which proved our Lord's greatest shame.

In the redemptive phase of the Cross the Lord did not, and could not, call His loved ones to any union with Him-

self; that is, we could not share with Him in the expiation
of sin. He does, however, call us into the fellowship of other
aspects of His Cross, and this we need to understand. In
our unregenerate state the problems which we encountered
pertained to sin, the world, Satan, and our corrupt natural
life. In deliverance from them we were identified with our
Lord in His sufferings and death and thus met some marks
of the Cross both in salvation and in the development of
Christian life. But the deep experience of being identified
with the Lord in this, the despite of both man and God,
is something foreign to us in early and immature Christian
life and experience.

So we find the Lord saying, "Open to me," implying a
new call to His loved one to open the heart still further to
Him and to receive Him now as one covered with the drops
of the night. She needed to learn at this stage an experience
of the deeper shame of the Cross and what it meant to be
despised by God. He addressed her as "My sister" — indicating that divine life was within her; "My love" — indicating
that she had knowledge of God's purpose; "My dove" — indicating that the Holy Spirit was present within her; "My
undefiled" — indicating the holiness, chastity, and dedication of her life. But here, however, He did not call her "My
spouse," because He would pause and wait to see her response to this fuller demand — whether or not the true nature
of the bride would be fully manifested. This response would
be her willingness for such complete union that she would
share even a reproach of shame with her Bridegroom-Lover.

Thus the Lord sought from her an open door to a new
revelation. Oh, yes, she had formerly opened her heart to
Him to receive Him as King of her life. Now the Lord
desired her, of her own volition, to receive Him as "Man
of sorrows, and acquainted with grief." We see in this deep
matter how the Lord desired to lead His loved one into the
fellowship of His sufferings and a following in His steps so
that she would become conformed to His death. The Lord,
however, would not compel her to walk that path. There
would be no pressure against her will. He would only knock
at her door and there entreat her until she became willing
of her own accord.

The *second* matter is the maiden's excuses. This call is something which passes the believer's understanding for a time. Most are unaware of the fact that the Cross includes an aspect of shame. They are not unfamiliar with some experience of the Cross, and, indeed, may well have suffered for its testimony in that they have been persecuted and put to shame by the malice of men. That kind of despite they found to be their glory, their hope, their life, and their power. They gloried in it. Never did they imagine for a moment that the Cross in which they gloried could ever become their personal shame. And this shame is not the loss of merely a worldly name or reputation, but the loss of even their spiritual fame so that men come to regard them as having been "smitten of God, and afflicted."

The Lord would now take the believer, represented by this maiden, through a period of testing in which there would be neither the comfort nor sympathy of friends and acquaintances but, on the contrary, misunderstanding by them as one rebuked and scolded by God. True enough, such a one might have experienced beforetimes the shame of the world, but never this kind of spiritual reproach. Such chagrin and misunderstanding would lead to deep questionings as to the relationship between the believer and God. Why forsaken, apparently, of God? It is in this that the believer comes to the realization of what is referred to in Colossians 1:24, to "fill up that which is behind [lacking] of the afflictions of Christ in my flesh for his body's sake, which is the church."

What a wondrous new calling is this? How deep, but oh, how cruel! No wonder the loved maiden shrank from it. She might have pondered and thought within herself such thoughts as these: "Is not the glory of God the most important of all things? And I have dedicated myself to Him and planned to serve Him for His own glory. If He now takes me into an experience where I am misunderstood and robbed of my good name and reputation among men, and if He causes me to be confounded as though there was something wrong between me and God, then how can He be glorified?"

Perhaps in this experience she was actually and honestly

more concerned for the glory of God than for what would happen to herself. This is the stripping of the Cross, and it goes on until she is stripped to a place where even her very concern for the glory of God has to go too. The Cross must strike to the very root of natural life until the believer is willing to accept whatever lot or portion is assigned by the Lord and allow God to take care of His own glory.

There was something more. To this loved one, to whom had come this deeper call of fellowship, there loomed another dilemma because of her concern for the work of God. In the past, because of her advanced knowledge of the Cross, she had drawn to herself many who had desired to know the way of the Lord more perfectly. Thus her very experience of the Cross-life had made her as a river of life to guide those who would follow on to know the Lord. Now, however, if she responds and accepts this new call and allows herself to be brought to a place of shame and contempt, would it not mean a loss of position and influence in His service and a diminishing of opportunity to serve Him? Truly, in former times it was her very experience of the Cross which drew others to her for help and guidance, but now, would not the shame and contempt of the Cross drive them away from her? How would anyone ever come near her again to learn the way of the Lord? Thoughts such as these, perhaps, gave rise to a new conflict within her and brought her to a dilemma of no small degree.

Her response, therefore, was a delaying excuse.

"I have put off my coat; how shall I put it on?" (5:3a).

In other words: "In my outward life and behavior the Cross has already stripped away that which was an expression of my old nature and manner of life. Why, then, must I now arise to accept this peculiar shame and solitude of the Cross, and so give rise to misunderstandings in the minds of others, as though I am putting on a garment that I had once discarded? Is it not enough to have such an experience of the Cross which effectively puts off the old creation?" This was her reasoning.

It is at this stage that many believers do not comprehend the two aspects of the Cross, one of which is negative and the other positive. To many, the Cross is known only on the negative side which strips the believer of the old ways and life. The attention of the maiden was focused in this instant on this very aspect that the Cross had indeed dealt with the old creation. But she did not understand the application and use of the Cross as a means of bringing her into Christ's triumphant life which had conquered death and "him that had the power of death, that is the devil." She perceived only the application of the Cross which had dealt with the works done in fleshly energy.

She did not understand, however, how the Cross governed the service in the new walk, and actually made such service possible. No doubt her misunderstanding was that such a positive service belonged to the resurrection side of the Cross and therefore was beyond the Cross. She did not realize that such service is the expression of the positive aspect of the Cross and that the Cross imprints on that new creation a brand of shame, suffering, and misunderstanding. The life of the Lord Jesus was originally the life of the new creation, yet was He not branded in His blessed body with all these marks by the Cross?

"I have washed my feet; how shall I defile them?" (5:3b).

Not only had her whole body been bathed — that is, her life fully cleansed and purified from sins—but also the dust and dirt and defilements of the world which soil believers had been faithfully attended to and cleansed away each day. It is evident that she maintained a constant cleansing so that no defilement of the world would leave upon her the appearance of digression, when all her desire was toward progression. Here again, we see that her attention was solely directed to keeping a clean state, which is negative only. She failed to grasp the fact that the defilement of which she was afraid in rising up to open her door for the Lord was no defilement at all. Her apology simply shows that there is a good which can be the enemy of the best—a good measure of identification with Christ which is not the fullest and which can be satisfied short of the highest.

Actually, the crux of the matter in hand was simply a revelation of the fact that she had become self-complacent with the good measure of experience already known of Christ, without realizing the importance of reaching out for what is spoken by Paul in Philippians 3:10: "That I may know him, and the power of his resurrection, and the fellowship of his sufferings, being made conformable unto his death." Unknowingly, a subtle form of self-consideration had crept in again which robbed her of exercise in going after Him. By reason of her past rich experiences, both in life and in services, all of which were for the glory of God, she had come to be regarded as having a position of leadership and authority in spiritual matters, and this question of hers really showed her unwillingness to alter her spiritual status. But this new call of the Lord Jesus was directed specifically to disturb that very state of affairs.

Indeed, all spiritual progress must necessarily involve a change from whatever is a present status and order of things. The willingness for change is precisely the price of progress. To covet, or to rest in, spiritual complacency at any time must always and forever mean a refusal to be motivated to a still higher calling. Whenever we thus become spiritually complacent, our conscience quietens down and does not inform us of our faults. Indeed, there seems to be nothing evil to trouble the conscience. And while many of our spiritual experiences undoubtedly may yet be derived from the death and resurrection of our Lord, we nevertheless find that the keen edge is taken off any further exploration of Christ's great purpose for us. Things which fall into a settled way of life usually do not demand further effort to seek anything new. Rather, we begin to fear that further search may rob us of enjoyment of our present peace. That is a perilous mistake, and it puts our Lord out in the cold and wet of the night.

The *third* matter to note is her opening of the door.

"My beloved put in his hand by the hole of the door, and my bowels were moved for him. I rose up to open to my beloved; and my hands dropped with myrrh, and my fingers with sweet smelling myrrh, upon the handles of the lock" (5:4-5).

The question here with the loved maiden was not one of refusal but of the infirmity of the flesh. Heretofore, her will had been completely committed to the Lord, but this sort of delay revealed her natural way of doing things—her customary way of life—her slowness to act. Actually there was within her a total absence of any other question whatsoever except the need for outward strength. Had there been defection on her part, or any serious falling away in spiritual affections, or any hardness of heart, she certainly would not have moved to open the door.

Thus the Lord "put in his hand by the hole of the door." This whole movement on His part was a calling of her into a deeper fellowship of His Cross, and not a chastisement for spiritual neglect. This was the hand which had embraced her, the hand which had been placed so tenderly under her head, the hand that was a nail-scarred hand. The Lord now once again employed this same hand to make His appeal to her and to entreat her to follow Him into this deeper fellowship. Putting His hand by the door's window inferred that the Lord did all that was possible to make Himself known in this peculiar revelation to her by means of this single part of His body. By the use of His hand He would remind her of Himself, for His scarred hand was a representation of what was in His heart—a revelation of His real and true Self.

Generally speaking, all our spiritual experiences and exercises are the outcome of being drawn by Christ. No deliverance from any state of complacency is possible except by first beholding a new revelation of, and entreaty by, the Lord Jesus Christ Himself. It is only then that we are moved to take a forward step in response to Him, and so to walk further with Him. Surely for one who has met and known Him there could only be a feeling for Him. Yet how few today are really moved as this maiden was by His approach and entreaty! Equally few in number are those who can discriminate and distinguish between being moved by the preaching of the Word and being moved by the Lord Himself.

The loved maiden then rose to open the door. Having been exercised by His appeal, she was now willing to abandon every excuse and embrace the shame of the Cross as her portion. Such was her determination now as she put forth her hand to open the door. When she says, "My hands dropped with myrrh, and my fingers with sweet smelling myrrh," she intended to show that there was now present upon her person not only the power but the fragrance of the Lord's death. It was as though she was now holding in her hand as a personal possession that life of Christ which had passed through death, and that life, rising like a tide within her, moved and stirred her to open the door. She must go the whole way with Him. The lock upon the door was her own will, but even now the handles of this were permeated with the sweet fragrance of His death.

Then, *fourth,* we note the Beloved withdrew and hid Himself from her.

"I opened to my beloved; but my beloved had withdrawn himself, and was gone: my soul failed when he spake [or "for his word"]: I sought him, but I could not find him; I called him, but he gave me no answer" (5:6).

To one who in times past, for lack of response, had been dealt with by the Lord in a very personal way, God's chastisement was surprisingly absent in this circumstance. The answer, no doubt, is that with mature believers His discipline is withheld until after the response of obedience is made. Only after response is made does such a one understand how shameful such disobedience or lack of response is. In the earlier stages of spiritual experience chastisement comes before obedience, and its purpose is to provoke obedience. It continues until there is obedience. But to the mature believer, chastisement or discipline follows after the act of obedience when he discovers the bitterness resulting from that complacent spirit which has failed to go along with the Lord.

There was a feeling of alarm in the loved maiden now that her Beloved was lost again. In the past she had lost His sensible presence due to her ignorance, but now her distress was of an intensely spiritual nature. It was as if her spirit had become enveloped and surrounded with a pall of darkness—an experience in which there was no glimmer of light. She now recalled the time when He had called her and how her soul had gone out towards Him.

Thus, for some unknown reason, she resented herself. Why couldn't her outward strength be a counterpart to her inward spirit? Why did hypocritical excuses for lack of outward strength arise, causing the Lord to hide the glory of His face? And what could she do in this dilemma but be moved again to seek Him anew and call after Him! But He was nowhere to be found. He answered not. Her seeking at this stage differed entirely from her seekings after Him in times past. She was not now on the street or in the broad ways of the city, but, rather, in the very presence of God. Yet even her prayer seemed of no avail. This was a new and altogether deeper exercise.

The *fifth* matter to observe is the wounding of the maiden.

"The watchmen that went about the city found me, they smote me, they wounded me; the keepers of the walls took away my veil from me" (5:7).

This time she did not seek out the watchmen as on a former occasion. To them she had become one of very beautiful features—one who had been greatly transformed. It was puzzling to them, too, how such a mature one could lose her Beloved. It may be that they had some desire to assist her. but their conversation and counsel brought her only pain and suffering. She needed consolation from them, but received nothing but rebuke. How well Mrs. Penn-Lewis in this connection quoted Psalm 69:26, "For they persecute him whom thou hast smitten; and they talk to the grief of those whom thou hast wounded."

The watchmen actually did not know how to help one in such a dilemma as this. If the Lord were hidden from her, then they concluded that she must be in the wrong somewhere. Little did they realize what she suffered because of such misunderstanding by them. Presuming that a scolding would help, they then berated her with words like sharp, piercing weapons. At this moment, therefore, she could really cry out the words of Psalm 69:20, "Reproach hath broken my heart; and I am full of heaviness: and I looked for some to take pity, but there was none; and for comforters, but I found none."

They "took away my veil from me." Thus there was no seeming end to her suffering. Not only were help and comfort denied her, but what had happened to her now brought her into open derision. Those who were the watchmen of the Lord, far from covering her from public reproach, now began to expose her and thus to broadcast her supposed failure. They were the very ones who treated her roughly and unjustly by taking away her covering, thus putting her to open shame and chagrin. Actually, they were making public news of her supposed failure, so that, as with Job of old, every friend from whom she expected some desired help turned out to be one who condemned her.

This group of watchmen were responsible leaders of the House of God. From the standpoint of spiritual qualification they should have been the ones with the ability to counsel her. Yet it is often the case that persons considered to be spiritual are the very ones who misunderstand and misrepresent another fellow-believer. We see, then, that the attitude of responsible brethren may be wrong, but the expression of this wrongness may also be permitted to fall upon us by the permissive will of God in order that we may know where we come short. When our relationship with the Lord is not stagnant, but progressive and moving in His will, then the Lord can hold the sceptre of His rule over such zealous brethren and deal with them. But if such a one as this loved maiden has come to a place where she is at a standstill and there is no onward progress, then He may permit the misunderstandings of brethren to deal roughly and ruthlessly with that one—more so than He Himself would deal with us.

Then, *sixth,* we see her seeking help from the daughters of Jerusalem.

"I charge you, O daughters of Jerusalem, if ye find my beloved, that ye tell him, that I am sick of love" (5:8).

When she failed to find the needed help from men of spiritual calibre, she now turned with her request to those who were spiritually less mature than herself. She had come to the realization that a complacent spirit had resulted in the Lord's withdrawal of the light of His countenance. In utter helplessness she thought that even the daughters of Jerusalem might be of some assistance to her—at least more sympathetic than the watchmen. What she says to them is, in effect, "I have failed. If at all feasible, please pray for me."

So deep was her exercise and perception about her sense of failure that she felt that even babes in the Lord might be qualified to assist her—so desperate was her plight. She was aware of their immaturity and imperfect union with the

Lord. It is her awareness of their poor state which brings forth the doubtful remark "If ye find Him." She knew well enough that they would have difficulty finding Him, but, in the midst of such overwhelming remorse and desperate need of help, she anticipates that there might be one or two among these daughters of Jerusalem who could give her spirit some encouragement. Her own prayer seemed definitely blocked, so she could only abandon herself to lean on others. The message she flashed out was, "I am sick of [with] love."

This statement was a second utterance of the same words, but the two utterances were made in entirely different circumstances. In the former time she was going along in the stream of love; in the present she was in a very dry period. To speak like this at a time of deep and surging emotion was understandable, but to speak such words at a time of straitening and intense adversity, darkness, and unsatisfied longing was most unusual. It proved that her life of faith had made a great step forward. She had learned to control environment and govern her own emotions. This love-sickness did not stem from having drunk and being full, but from a very deep hunger and thirst for the love of her Beloved. She is now overcome with tremendous longing for Him.

A *seventh* consideration is the question arising from these daughters of Jerusalem.

"What is thy beloved more than another beloved, O thou fairest among women? . . . that thou dost so charge us?" (5:9).

Although these daughters of Jerusalem did not possess the full life of the new creation, they were such as could recognize the superior quality of the life in this loved maiden— her spiritual beauty: remarkable humility in the new-creation life, her holy character, and her touch of glory. These were features recognized by them as worthy of praise and commendation, even though they themselves did not bear such virtues. It was true that at this moment she had lost the light of her Beloved's countenance, but she was still "the fairest among women"—the most beauteous of beauties, for she possessed that beauty which could not pass away.

By way of comparison, Christ, her Beloved, has *no* rival in the matter of perfections of character. *None* can compare with Him. It is the case, however, with some who have not the mature intelligence and affections of the bride, that they inevitably do compare Him with other men. As they see things, the Lord Jesus is not an absolute in the perfection of His humanity. Thus they fail to know Him merely by making comparisons or by means of contrast. This Beloved did indeed excel far above all other beloveds. But this very question from the daughters of Jerusalem revealed the fact that, though they may have been in the system of grace, they had not been given, as yet, that intimate revelation of the Lord Himself. They needed, therefore, to learn more of Him from the reflected light shining through this maiden.

Then, in the *eighth* place, we have her personal impressions of her Beloved. J. N. Darby thinks the implication here is obvious. Whenever the bride talks about the perfections of the Bridegroom-Lover, she is always assured of His glad approval. It is usually to others that she expresses her impressions and feelings concerning Him and seldom directly to Him. On the contrary, when He speaks about her He invariably does so directly to her and is spontaneously free and perfectly at ease in doing so. He lets her know of His delight in her. When we consider Christ and our relationship with Him, how truly beautiful and appropriate this is!

Aroused by their question, the maiden breathed out her impressions of her Beloved. Thus the Lord awakened in her the former revelations which would reveal His image with brightness. By recalling His features known to her in times past she would be spontaneously revived in her appreciation of Him in the present.

One thing is very remarkable; namely, the revelation which we formerly received of the Lord Jesus through the Holy Spirit can sometimes become very hazy, but can never be completely lost. This beloved maiden, no matter what the present difficulty may be, was still the superior counsellor of those represented by the daughters of Jerusalem. Her exercises in trial were still better than their apparent victory.

Her first statement is in verse 10:

"My beloved is white [radiant] and ruddy, the chiefest among ten thousand."

This was a kind of general description. It speaks of His godliness and how far separate He was from sinners. The "white" of Him was not pale white, or death white, but "white and ruddy"—the ruddy complexion of perfect health. This indicated that He was vibrant with fulness of life and power, and like David who "was ruddy, and withal of a beautiful countenance, and goodly to look to" (I Samuel 16:12). It was the health glow of youth. We can see how, in the higher realms of spiritual life, the Lord makes Himself known to be full of the power of life, even having upon Him the glow of eternal youth. From the time when He was in the temple at twelve years of age until the day when He was seated in heaven at the right hand of the Father, He never displayed at any time the loss of any strength or power.

It is thus that He is known as "the chiefest among ten thousand," that is, as the One to whom all His people rally. Christ was, and forever is, the banner of His people, whom they lift high in hope as we see in Isaiah 59:19: "When the adversary shall come in like a flood, the Spirit of Jehovah will lift up a banner against him" (Darby). The banner means the Cross. The Lord Jesus was the One lifted high as a banner — "the Lamb that was slain" — but wherever His Name is proclaimed tens of thousands rally to Him. None can rival Him. He is to His saints "the chiefest among ten thousand."

After this general proclamation of her over-all impression she now analyzes the impression she received by the Spirit of the Lord.

"His head is as the most fine gold" (5:11a).

This is a description of His divine attributes. He possessed God's life and God's glory. "For in him dwelleth all the fulness of the Godhead bodily" (Colossians 2:9). This Christ, established by God as the Head over all things, has all of God dwelling in Him. There is nothing in God which is not in Him. Therefore we hold Him "the Head, from which all the body by joints and bands having nourishment ministered, and knit together, increaseth with the increase of God" (Colossians 2:19).

"His locks are bushy, and black as a raven" (5:11b).

"Black as a raven" is an indication of His everlasting vigor

and power. He manifests Himself as the One with everlasting
locks of hair. The black hair in this impression of Him
speaks of that vigor of His eternal life which can never
deteriorate or wane. True, when the strength of life in one
begins to decline, the Scriptures describe such as having a
hoary head. "Gray hairs are here and there upon him, yet
he knoweth [it] not" is Hosea's apt illustration of Ephraim's
unconscious loss of spiritual power. The Lord Jesus, however, did not have a single thread of white in His hair as this
loved maiden viewed Him. There was the abiding freshness
of eternal life—"Jesus Christ the same yesterday, today, and
forever" (Heb. 13:8).

**"His eyes are as the eyes of doves by the rivers of waters,
washed with milk, and fitly set" (5:12).**

Eyes are the seat of expression, and this description also
speaks of an intimacy known by His spouse. Words and
letters are also means of communication, but they are for
those at a distance or in a far-off country. The expression
in the eyes is for those who are very close, and here we learn
how near this loved maiden had come to Him when she
could describe such expression. The Holy Spirit came upon
the Lord as a dove, and the most beautiful feature of a dove
is its eyes. It was the Spirit's anointing which made the Lord's
eyes so tender in their expression of love to His loved one.

"By the rivers of waters," or brooks, signifies the shining
sparkle of those eyes. They glistened with tender affection.
"Washed with milk" means that His inward thoughts shining through were so pure that they had a purifying effect
upon her. It is also said that His eyes were "fitly set"
or, as we may say, well-positioned or properly located, and
this indicates that He viewed her with great favor and understanding. Thus the eyes of the Lord are His instruments of
tender expression toward those believers who go on, as did
this maiden, to mature affections. To such, His eyes are as
beautiful as doves' eyes—full of life, free from disease or
pollution, expressing pure thoughts of love and focusing with
well-proportioned vision. Thus He was never in danger of
seeing wrongly or seeing the wrong thing.

"His cheeks are as a bed of spices, as sweet flowers" (5:13a).
These same cheeks had undergone much shame and des-

pite. "I gave my back to the smiters, and my cheeks to them that plucked off the hair: I hid not my face from shame and spitting" (Isaiah 50:6). His cheeks, also, were made the butt of men's derision: "And they spit upon him, and took the reed, and smote him on the head" (Matthew 27:30). No wonder, then, that such a believer as this one looked upon His cheeks as a bed of fragrant spices or scented herbs.

"His lips like lilies, dropping sweet smelling myrrh" (5:13b).

The "lilies" referred to here speak of kingly glory, as in Matthew 6:28-29: "Consider the lilies of the field . . . even Solomon in all his glory was not arrayed like one of these." How glorious were the teachings of Christ! And how sweet were the words which dropped from His lips! They were of sweet savor, like drops of myrrh, for "Never man spake like this man" (John 7:46), and "all bare him witness, and wondered at the gracious words which proceeded out of his mouth" (Luke 4:22): as the Psalmist said, "Grace is poured into thy lips" (Psalm 45:2). No wonder, then, that men so praised Him and were amazed at His speech.

Moreover, these drops of myrrh not only indicate the fragrance of graciousness, but also the identification which this one had with Him in His death. The implication is that in her life His death stood out in clear tones in its outworking. The drops of myrrh which fell from His lips and all that He uttered in words of grace and blessing came to her because of His death on the Cross. Whether such words proclaimed "Thy sins be forgiven," or "Go in peace," or "Believe and live," or "Rise and walk"—all such wonderful and gracious words were spoken on the strength of His redeeming death on the Cross.

"His hands are as gold rings set with the beryl" (5:14a).

The word "rings" is the same Hebrew word as "folding" (or "pivoting") in I Kings 6:34, and this suggests that their aim never fluctuates off course nor is their purpose lost. "Gold" stands for Divinity. These rings of gold hold or enfold her in a divine way for the fulfillment of the purpose of God in her. "Beryl" is mentioned a number of times in the Old Testament, for instance, in Ezekiel 1:16: "The appearance of the wheels and their work was like unto the colour of a beryl," and also in Daniel 10:6: "His body also was like the beryl."

Both these verses carry the idea of firm establishment. In Ezekiel's vision we see how the gentle power of Christ, expressed in the throne having "the appearance of a man above upon it," was in the place of rule, yet these wheels of God's government were always turning. Later, in Daniel, we see the Lord Christ with a body like beryl still sustaining and directing the affairs of His people and moving them through to final consummation. The rings of gold set with beryl, then, spoke of the strength of His hands to establish firmly and bring to completion the purposes of God.

"His belly is as bright ivory overlaid with sapphires" (5:14b).

The word "belly" is better understood as the seat of the emotions, being identical with the word for deep feeling found in chapter 5:4 where she said: "My bowels were moved for him." The verse carries the inference that the Lord Jesus, too, was a Person rich with the deepest sensibilities, that He was moved with great feelings of love for His people. "Ivory," unlike the lifeless gem, is obtained from the elephant's tusk. Ivory is the product of pain and indicated that His love for her was born out of His sufferings unto death as a Sin-bearer. The deep feelings for His people were nurtured within His super-sensitive life because of the greatness of the suffering and death He underwent for them. These feelings being "overlaid with sapphires" are pictures of carvings on the ivory which speak of delicate and exquisite craftsmanship and picture many facets of His feelings.

All these carvings combined to show that His loving and tender feelings were neither superficial nor casual. They were "overlaid with sapphires," indicating heavenly clearness as in Exodus 24:10: "And they saw the God of Israel: and there was under his feet as it were a paved work of a sapphire stone, and as it were the body of heaven in his clearness." These sapphires were overlaid upon and around all His deepest feelings; hence, when those feelings of love moved out to His loved one, how heavenly and transcendent did they appear!

"His legs are as pillars of marble, set upon sockets of fine gold" (5:15a).

The feet, Scripturally speaking, refer to walk or movement; but only His legs are mentioned here and they signify

His power to stand. The word for "marble" is exactly the same as that which is translated in other scriptures as "fine linen" and this points to our Lord's inherent righteousness. His legs being as "pillars" speak of His stability. Thus she speaks of her Beloved in all that He was in Himself, and all that He had established in the strength of His righteousness, as having immovable stability. There was nothing in His life or work which could be the least bit shaken. This is the impression left upon all who, like this loved maiden, follow Him fully. Thrice she has mentioned "fine gold," as at different times she has referred to the thoughts of His mind, and the works of His hands, and now here to the stability of His steps. The gold in Scripture is always indicative of the Divine nature, the attributes of God. Thus we are led to see that it was God who was expressing Himself through His Son, sustaining Him in all His ways, and finding full satisfaction and delight in Him through His perfect yieldedness.

"His countenance [appearance] is as Lebanon, excellent as the cedars" (5:15b).

High above the levels and standards of earth was this Blessed One who dwelt in the high and lofty heavenlies. Everything around Him was of a heavenly nature. "Excellent as the cedars" shows something of His elevated character. Though a Man, yet He was now a Man glorified in the heights of heaven. As the tall and stately cedars tower and transcend all other trees, so likewise was the Lord singularly exalted as the One Man whom the Father honored and glorified.

"His mouth is most sweet: yea, he is altogether lovely" (5:16a).

The word in the original is better translated "palate of taste" and is similar to the word in 2:3, "his fruit was sweet to my taste." This is very different from what is meant by the mouth. It speaks of a certain aspect of His mediatorial work. Everything which proceeded from God the Father was first tasted by Him before passing it to us. All that was from God was first stored up and deposited in His Son before He sent it forth to us. His was the true work of a Mediator. How very sweet it all is! When we fully know Him, we cannot help but testify that all that ever came to us from God did indeed first come through His dear Son.

At this point the heart of the true believer cannot but be warmly stirred and moved in admiration of the one who could utter such high words of praise about Him. We may well stay here for a moment to review the path trodden, and reflect upon Him whom we have confessed as our Lord. How could one do other than cry with this maiden, "He is altogether lovely." No matter what part of His life and character we may speak about, we must conclude that He is altogether lovely. And those who wholeheartedly follow Him proudly say with this maiden, "This is my Beloved, and this is my Friend, and can you blame me for seeking after Him?"

Such was her impression of the Lord and such her intimate knowledge of Him and her appreciation of all she had received of Him. Here such a description is an indication of the closeness of her union with Him and the **depth** of communion enjoyed in His company. Of a truth, she had with open face beheld as in a glass the glory of the Lord and was being changed into His very image, from glory to glory.

In conclusion we may say that her words expressed a profound depth of feeling, as though the full blaze of the sun had flooded her soul within until she just had to burst out in her address to the daughters of Jerusalem with this loud glad song of praise:

"He is altogether lovely. This is my beloved, and this is my friend" (5:16b).

The *ninth* matter in this section concerns these daughters of Jerusalem. They now ask the loved maiden,

"Whither is thy beloved gone, O thou fairest among women? whither is thy beloved turned aside? that we may seek him with thee" (6:1).

Having heard the aforementioned testimony, these now desired to go out themselves in search of Him. This was a very natural sequence of events after hearing such testimony. In the loved maiden they had seen one in whom was the full effect of the new-creation work. She was filled with the freshness of that new-creation life. In her appreciation she had proclaimed the Christ she knew experientially, and this was so different from their own mere intellectual approach to Him. No wonder there was about her a sense of power— a peculiar drawing power. No wonder they continued to

praise her as "the fairest among women"—the supremely
beautiful among beautiful ones. At the same time they expressed their own awakened desire to join her in spiritual
search and inquiry.

The question which troubled them, however, was this: If
He were altogether lovely, then where could He have gone
and how could He have hidden Himself from them? They
repeatedly enquired of her as to His whereabouts so they
could find Him in the same way, implying that if they could
not do so then He must be estranged from her, too. In this
kind of questioning they had more than a suggestion that she
knew Him to be altogether lovely. She ought to know
exactly where to locate Him for them and guide them to
Him, now that they desired to seek Him with her. They had,
you see, been deeply impressed and stirred by the manner
in which she exulted in her Beloved, and this was so unlike
what any other thought of Him.

Finally, there is the bride's response to the daughters of
Jerusalem.

**"My beloved is gone down into his garden, to the beds of
spices, to feed in the gardens, and to gather lilies" (6:2).**

She had been seeking spiritual succor from the immature
daughters of Jerusalem. In doing so she had hoped to discover from them the whereabouts of her Beloved. But suddenly, while relating to them that glowing description of
His glorious Person, enlightenment had come, and she understood where her Beloved really was to be found.

Thus there came forth from her a very definite knowledge
of Him. "My beloved is gone down into his garden, to the
beds of spices, to feed in the gardens, and to gather lilies."
This garden of His was but figurative language of her own
life in Christ. He was living in her own spiritual affections.
The reality of this had already become clear to her in 4:12,
16, and 5:1. It simply meant that very suddenly inner light
had shone and brought clarity of understanding about His
indwelling Presence. The Beloved had not really left her,
nor was it necessary for her to ascend into Heaven or descend into Hades to seek Him. He was near her and within
—as Paul says in Romans 10:8: "in thy mouth, and in thy
heart."

During the interval of her delayed response to His latest call to deeper identification, He seemed almost to have departed from her. But this is only part of His ways. He withdraws from the area of conscious feeling in His loved one in order that she might be more alive to the value of His presence. In truth He still possessed her heart and dwelt within it. In such withdrawals He would also teach her not to be fretful nor over-exercised about the lack of conscious feelings. Rather would He have her make confession of any failure of response and ask for forgiveness. Then, to counteract any suggestions that He had left her, she should lay hold of His Word of promise to her and do so with quietness and confidence, knowing that He is always present in His own garden. At His own appointed time He will surely once again manifest His living presence and make her conscious of Himself.

When feelings of estrangement come, therefore, He would teach us all how to rest in His enduring Word and sink into the faithfulness of all such words of promise. His faithfulness far exceeded hers, and to seek Him in the strength of mere fleshly activity would never bring the realization of His presence. Indeed, such seekings invariably end in confusion to the seeker. Thus we learn that while failure to respond to the Lord's deepest calls may inflict deep wounds upon the life of the believer, yet to seek Him in the activity of the flesh only inflicts deeper ones.

The steps of her recovery are clear. First, it was through her own spoken description and appreciation of every phase of her Beloved's glorious Person. Her hesitation to respond when He had called her into deeper identification did not deter her in this nor cause her to consider it the least incongruous to speak of His excellence and faithfulness. Unknowingly, by this exercise of praise to His peerless worth, she was led out of herself, and this deliverance from this subtle form of self-life now brought her the knowledge of His whereabouts. He was within her affections and central to all her hopes. It is therefore the consideration of His Divine Person —His grace and truth, His faithfulness and love—by which, all unknowingly, we find recovery of that light we may have lost for a time.

You can see, too, that in this state of exercise she still continued to do her best for others and to answer their inquiries. Though she herself seemed to have lost something of His immediate fellowship, yet it remained her burden that these less-mature daughters of Jerusalem might discover how precious He is and that they, too, might be stirred to seek more intimate fellowship with Him. What she was recounting in her testimonial of Him was the revelation she had formerly received of Him. And is it not true that, as believers gather to talk about their Lord, He is in very close proximity and listening with a pleased ear? And surely at that very time of speaking His worth, He will spontaneously reveal Himself in living presence.

It was so with this loved one. Though she herself hungered and thirsted for Him, yet as she endeavored to satisfy others, she herself found satisfaction in return. Here, then, we see how once again she was delivered from these new challenges of self-life. In her delayed response to Him, symptoms of spiritual darkness and decline began to appear again; but when drawn away from herself by an expressed appreciation and exaltation of her Beloved, these symptoms quickly vanished.

As this new spiritual intelligence began to break upon her, she was seemingly addressing the daughters of Jerusalem. Actually it was a kind of soliloquy. She was speaking out her thoughts as though these friends were present with her. Although she had sensed some estrangement with her Beloved, yet she had now discovered that, in this long period in which she had been without sensible impressions of His presence, He was nevertheless in His garden. "Garden" here is singular and signifies the loved one herself, which simply means He had actually become more deeply involved and resident in her life.

But He also found some measure of satisfaction in other "gardens." The word here is plural and indicates the lives of other, though less mature, saints. "Beds of spices" have been mentioned previously as referring to the cheeks. Thus we find the Lord presenting Himself to the inner life of His people and finding no place to compare with those bridal affections, but also finding some outward fruits in many of His saints and a measure of spiritual beauty to admire in all. The Lord is present in the hearts of all His people to shepherd them and to supply each need and also "to gather lilies," by which is meant that which expresses the pure flower of that life first derived from Himself.

"I am my beloved's, and my beloved is mine: he feedeth among the lilies" (6:3).

When she came to such understanding as this, there came also a realization that though feelings change, the covenant between the Beloved and herself was of an unchangeable character and forever held steadfast. Thus she declares with full assurance and confidence: "I am my beloved's, and my beloved is mine." In former times, when she was experientially on a more superficial level and exuberent with highly emotional feelings, she had said, "My beloved is mine, and I am his" (2:16). The former expression was founded largely on emotional feelings, but the latter rests solidly on faith alone. This spontaneous expression from the heart has clearly moved the focus of life from self to the glorious Person of the Lord Jesus Himself.

As of old He was still found to be "feeding among the lilies." By this is meant that He was ever leading and feeding His flock in pure places. Where it was His custom to lead and feed them, He was still doing so. Through this deep exercise of spirit, then, she had learned to look only unto the one unchanging and eternal Lord, and not to follow willy-nilly after her rising and subsiding emotions. She could now rest in Him, not only amidst the enjoyments of everyday life, but also in time of adversity and when deprived of sensible feelings.

LIFE WITHIN THE VEIL (6:4-13)

In the *first* place there is new commendation by the Beloved (6:4-9). She could well expect that following this important spiritual exercise the Lord would spontaneously express His satisfaction in her. And this He did. We perhaps need to be reminded here of the theme of the *Song of Songs*, namely, a developing union with every forward step. The objective of union is communion, and communion is developed only by increased identification. Consequently, what she had beheld in the Person of the King was transforming her into the same character as that of the King. And likewise, what the King came to see in her person was the expression of Himself. His own glorious life was being personified in her personality. Thus the Lord, in commending such believers as represented by the Bride, does so because developing union with Himself increasingly exhibits in their characters the measure of life which they have received from Him.

"Thou art beautiful, O my love, as Tirzah, comely as Jerusalem, terrible as an army with banners" (6:4).

This is the Lord's evaluation and appreciation of His loved one as He looks at her in the light of the heavenly sanctuary. This is her hidden life within the veil—what she is in the Kingdom of the Father. For He has already spoken of her comeliness, both general and specific. Now He declares, "Thou art beautiful, O my love, as Tirzah, comely as Jerusalem." "Tirzah," meaning "delight," was the King's residential palace and answers to the Holy Place in heaven, which is God's abiding place. "Jerusalem" was the chosen vessel through which God manifests His glory and which is the center of all His activity. When John saw the New Jerusalem, he called it "the holy city" and likened its beauty to that of "a bride adorned for her husband" (Rev. 21:2) Thus we see the Lord looking upon His loved one as she is in her heavenly position before God, and in her life as she lives it in that realm which is of God.

Whosoever is within that Jerusalem has nothing which is uncomely. Whosoever is within that Tirzah has nothing but what is beautiful. This is the Bride in her heavenly position before God and seen in her secret life in the Holy Place within the veil. Such ones as are represented by this bride begin even now to exhibit and express the future beauty and comeliness of life within the heavenly sanctuary.

"Terrible as an army with banners." The word "terrible" means fearful. In a time of war it is most important to have weapons. In the time of victory, however, it is important to have a banner to display. If there is defeat in combat, then the only thing to do is to roll up the banner and feel crestfallen. But an unfurled banner denotes glorious victory. Here, therefore, the phrase signifies that the loved maiden was not only beautiful and comely but strong like a heavenly host. And though she was serene and quiet as a sanctuary, yet she could brandish the glory of complete victory before all the wicked powers of hell and of men. Her life within the veil was not meant to be lived only in the sanctuary of God's presence but in the field of battle before the enemy.

It is in the realm of the heavenlies where the saints have their union with Christ, but it is also in that realm where they meet the real attack from enemy forces. God never intended that believers possess merely heavenly beauty and be without spiritual stamina to conduct warfare. Every battle with the enemy is remembered in the heavenly record. The Lord would have His saints possess not only the loveliness of spiritual features but also some of the "terrible" traits of character which make them the fear of their enemies.

It would appear that many believers today have lost both loveliness and terribleness before the hosts of darkness, and even before men. Are they afraid of us? The Scriptures often describe the Lord as being fearful, and this means that He is fearful toward His enemies because of His holy character. If we maintained a holy character and victorious warfare, we could witness enemy retreat before our eyes, and the hosts of opposition would move back and not dare advance upon us. Sacrificing this aspect of fearfulness, believers are feared neither by man nor by the devil.

"Turn away thine eyes from me, for they have overcome me" (6:5a).

This phrase is a poetic expression in which we see how strong her love for the Lord is. It is expressed through her eyes and, as it were, overwhelms Him. It does not mean that He is refusing her love or spurning it. The phrase indicates a commendation with a peculiar challenge in it. It is something like the Lord's turning for a moment from the Syrophenician woman in Mark 7:26-29, or His deliberate tarrying for two days when Martha and Mary had sent urgently for Him in John 11:6, or His word to Moses in Exodus 32:10, "Let me alone," or His plea to Jacob, "Let me go, for the day breaketh" in Genesis 32:26. So also in this verse. He seems to employ words which convey the idea of wanting to turn away.

But this is a move which is designed to challenge a return expression of love. The mention of her eyes has the thought, not of a passing glance, but of a riveted gaze which connotes the strength of love. The Lord conveys the idea that He is irresistibly overcome by the strength of such love. The real ways of the Lord are known by those who can look beyond His seeming rejection or delay or spurning to His appreciation of the strong affection in His saints.

"Thy hair is as a flock of goats that appear from Gilead. Thy teeth are as flock of sheep which go up from the washing, whereof every one beareth twins, and there is not one barren among them. As a piece of pomegranate are thy temples within thy locks" (6:5b-7).

The hair speaks of the strength of her dedication, as with the Nazarite. The reference to her teeth again points to her capacity to digest the spiritual truth. Her cheeks (temples) which are within her veil, reiterate her hidden beauty. Much of the commendation here echoes the praise which the Lord once spoke of her in 4:1-3, which now reveals two important facts.

First, the love of the Lord never changes. Though procrastination may be a constant temptation to this loved maiden in her many failures springing from darkness, yet the Lord's kind dealings with her remain ever the same. The Lord was ever desirous to remove every doubt in her concerning Himself and to free her from every illusion which might rise within her mind that He could ever change in His relation to her. Hence, once again He addressed her with these same words of commendation. How true it is that every time a believer fails, the first thing which disappears is invariably the confidence of faith, and in its place arises a misconception concerning the relationship between the believer and the Lord. Little do we realize what a bundle of doubts we are! It is against such doubts that these sweet words of commendation are directed.

In the second place, many experiences which come to us in the process of moving to higher levels of spiritual attainment should be kept and not discarded. These may include various dedications, increased capacity for spiritual light and truth, revelation concerning the hidden life, and such like. These all were vital in the process of development from an elementary to a more mature level. By reason of progress in development, however, the nature and character of some experiences change while that of others do not suffer change with progress.

At this present high level of experience unto which this loved one had come, there is a more profound depth to experience. For instance, in our own spiritual walk have we not known the experience of having to learn one lesson over and over again? And that which we finally learned through this repeated lesson was ultimately far more profound and perfect than that which the same lesson taught us in the elementary stage. The experience was something similar, but our capacity for learning spiritual lessons from that experience had vastly changed.

"There are threescore queens, and fourscore concubines, and virgins without number" (6:8).

All these are related in different ways to King Solomon. Looking at this from a mere worldly viewpoint it would, of course, be considered a great error to have so many lovers, but it is here to teach a spiritual truth and is a picture both profound and beautiful. The Lord desires to possess all believers in the fullest and purest of spiritual affections and in the closest and most intimate relationship. Corporately speaking, the bride of Christ is but one. Individually speaking, however, the measure of affections for Him and the character of relationship to Him differ in believers, and these differences are represented by the queens, the concubines, and the virgins. Adam, Isaac, and Moses are all prototypes of Christ, and their brides are figures of the Church in a corporate and complete sense.

But Solomon is a prototype of Christ in His relation to the individual believer. In his own personal life, Solomon is no picture at all of the Lord Jesus Christ, since he fell so far short in holiness of life and spiritual behavior. It is not in his personal and unrighteous conduct, but rather in his high and kingly office that he is a figure of Christ. In the Scriptures even a thief is used to represent one aspect of our Lord's movement, as in Matthew 24:43-44: " . . . if the goodman of the house had known in what watch the thief would come, he would have watched . . . Therefore be ye also ready: for in such an hour as ye think not the Son of man cometh." It is not in his thieving that the thief is likened unto the Lord but in the unexpectedness of his appearing. Whosoever is wise will understand this.

Individually speaking, then, the love relationship of believers to the Lord differs experientially. Some are such as can be represented by queens, others have a kind of concubine nature, and there are still others whose affections are like those of a simple and immature virgin. All these had a love relationship to the King, yet all fell short of that pursuit of the Lord characterized by the loved maiden, and none had her unique place in relationship.

"My dove, my undefiled is but one; she is the only one of her mother, she is the choice one of her that bare her. The daughters saw her, and blessed her; yea, the queens and the concubines, and they praised her" (6:9).

In this verse the Spirit of the Lord desires us to see that it is those who fully satisfy the Lord's heart who alone are to be regarded as "but one"—unique. It does not infer, of course, that there is only a single believer who ever reached such a state, but that all who come to spiritual fulness of affections are regarded as "only ones" in the eyes of the Lord. They are undoubtedly a special company who have a special place. This company, represented by this loved maiden, live in the Spirit. They are as a "dove" in the singleness of their eye for Christ, and "undefiled" in the sense of being completely separated unto Him. This company—represented by the bride and born of her mother, grace—has progressed and developed to fulness of love for the Lord Jesus. Thus as a complete expression of the working of grace she was "the choice one." This grace not only connoted the glorious forgiveness of sins by God, but all that is wrought in the heart through the years by His constant working.

Those, therefore, in whom God is able to do much are those who are ever open to receive much. Those in whom a lesser work is done are those who limit God's work of grace within them. God, indeed, is ever ready to bestow much grace and thus accomplish much work in believers, but not all permit Him liberty to carry on and complete His work in them. All that stems from self is of imposed law, but that which is of God is all of free grace. The Church is full of children of grace, but those who allow that grace to work to its full end and complete accomplishment are few and far between. Here, then, the King is not saying that such as this loved one is the only one begotten of grace. What He is saying is that here is "the choice one" of all thus begotten. All who belong to Him are begotten of Him, but here is one who has developed to be fully and wholly identified with Him.

"The daughters saw her, and blessed her; yea, the queens and the concubines, and they praised her." Many believers who are not fully mature themselves or wholly devoted to the Lord nevertheless do recognize those who are so. Although not of the same spiritual calibre, they possess a sufficient measure of the new-creation life to admire that complete yieldedness to Christ such as seen in this spouse. There are some who have such a degree of obedience in their own inner lives that they are able to appreciate and to commend the worth and beauty of one wholly committed to the Lord. From a mere physical point of view these daughters, queens, and concubines may not altogether approve or go along with this maiden, but on the basis of grace received they do realize how blessed she was. Her life within the veil and all that was expressed of God were exceedingly precious and much to be admired.

In the *second* place, we see something of her glory.

"Who is she that looketh forth as the morning, fair as the moon, clear as the sun, and terrible as an army with banners?" (6:10).

In this verse the Holy Spirit is again speaking through a third party—perhaps one of the queens or concubines— and employing an exclamatory question in order to bring out the glory of this loved maiden. All four parts of the question call attention to different aspects of her life in the Lord. In this way the Spirit of God challenges less mature believers to think. By means of interrogation He calls them to pay attention to the full work of God in the life of an advanced soul. They are thus brought to an understanding of what is pleasing and acceptable to the Lord. We have noticed before that when the Holy Spirit brought in this form of question it was invariably after the chosen bride had received some new revelation or edification. This was so in Chapter 3. You will find it to be so in Chapter 8. Here you have it in the present instance. This prompting or goading by means of interrogation is meant to lead immature believers into an understanding of the why and wherefore of those fuller spiritual affections manifest in the spouse.

"She that looketh forth as the morning." The chosen of the Lord have come to a new morning through grace. "Morning" here and "daybreak" in 2:17 are identical. At this stage her shadows have fled away, and there is no remaining darkness in her relation to Christ. She has now come to live the life of "nothing between." Although as yet she has not come to the full light of what life at high noon means, yet her life is like the womb of the morning. Her hopes shine with the brightness of daybreak. Her whole being has an outlook similar to the prospect of an opening day shining with morning light. The hope and the course of this new day is to move to the high noon of meridian glory, for "the path of the just is as the shining light, that shineth more and more unto the perfect day" (Proverbs 4:18). The path of the just in the hand of the Lord has high noon as its goal and nothing less. There can be no satisfying life from any other source than the full splendor of Christ.

"Fair as the moon." Here attention is directed not so much to the size of the moon but to its radiance and beauty. The moon shines with a soft and gentle light. It is in this figure that we see the bride of Christ to be a heavenly creation reflecting the light of the hidden Lord Jesus into the black night of earth so that those in moral and spiritual darkness may be illumined and find their paths by such faithful witness. This is the believer in his relation to the world. "It shall be established for ever as the moon, and as a faithful witness in heaven" (Psalm 89:37).

"Clear as the sun." This speaks of the absence of gloom and the fulness of heavenly light. Both the moon and the sun refer to aspects of the heavenly life of the spouse. The implication in the figure of the moon is that she is a recipient of grace, making her a heavenly body to shine upon the earth as a witness. The implication in the figure of the sun is that her life is the life of God, and with that heavenly life she lives her life in the Lord and in the Kingdom of the Father. On the one hand, she is, in herself, something dead, lifeless, and without atmosphere, as the moon is; but she has been made a new heavenly body and is in touch with the hidden sun, Christ, from whom she draws all her light to witness. As the moon faces the sun, there is light received and reflected. When it turns its back, so to speak, it is still there but there is no light with which to witness. On the other hand, from the viewpoint of the Father, she is in Christ and seen as a new creation indwelt with His Spirit, flooded with that light and the life of Christ, which she possesses and in which is no darkness at all. He is the Sun: so likewise she becomes a sun.

"Terrible as an army with banners." Not only was she filled with hope concerning the future, and not only in full possession of the heavenly life of Christ, but also one who, in relation to her enemies and every circumstance, was superabundantly triumphant. Her daily song was the song of victory. And we may well ask at this point, "Do you know this maiden? Have you seen her? Is this your image? Are you in possession of this glorious life in Christ?"

In the *third* place, we see something of her humility.

"I went down into the garden of nuts to see the fruits of the valley, and to see whether the vine flourished, and the pomegranates budded" (6:11).

Much embarrassed by this praise, the maiden turned her attention to other matters by going down to the nut orchard. Nuts—with their hard shells which require careful cracking before the delicious and nourishing interiors can be extracted —may be likened to the Word of God, which yields its soul-satisfying meats only to those who diligently, and with prayer, seek to rightly divide the word of truth (II Timothy 2:15). She also made an examination of the vines in the Lord's vineyard and an inspection of His pomegranate groves— which symbolize the many and varied works of ministry established by the Lord—so that she might become familiar with what her Beloved was doing in the orbit of the total visible Church. Rather than basking in praise, however deserved, we see that her thoughts were concerned with God's message and its outworking in the lives of others.

"Or ever [Before] I was aware, my soul made me like [set me among] the chariots of Ammi-nadib [which means, "my people of a willing heart"] (6:12).

While she was engrossed in this study of the Lord's Word and this investigation of His present-day works among the children of men, before she realized what was happening she found herself being carried by her Beloved in His chariot across the fields of earth. Their personal chariot was accompanied by others, all of which are spoken of as "the chariots of my people of a willing heart." This may be interpreted as a sudden rise of willing and ready affections, amidst fields which were lagging in fruits, of a superior kind of believer who recognizes the authority of the Monarch. They rose up in a day of declension as "a people of a willing heart" to provide a vehicle for the Lord's movements. "Thy people shall be willing in the day of thy power, in the beauties of holiness from the womb of the morning: thou hast the dew of thy youth" (Psalm 110:3). It is not the total Church that is represented in this "people of willing heart," for all are not so in these days. Rather, it is only a remnant, represented by the maiden, who have willing hearts for His work.

Then *fourth*, there is progress and victory.

"Return, return, O Shulamite; return, return, that we may look upon thee. What will ye see in the Shulamite? As it were the company of two armies" (6:13).

This passage opens with a call by some of the daughters of Jerusalem: "Return . . . that we may look upon thee!" To this others made reply, in effect: "Why do you wish to look upon this Shulamite? What do you see in her?" The answer is given in the following verses (7:1-5) in the form of a victory dance.

"Shulamite" means "a person of peace," and is Solomon's new way of writing about this loved maiden. The Holy Spirit is, by means of this request, earnestly entreating her to return and come into view in these end days so that others less mature might look upon her. She was indeed as a chariot, moving swiftly and progressively, going on from victory to victory, riding on with her Lord and with no impediment to her progress. But there were others who desired to observe her life and ways in order to ascertain the secret of her equipment for such progress and the way she could forge ahead without hindrance.

The appeal contained two inherent desires. First, it set forth the desire of those who were in genuine quest of full spiritual affections as seen in the spouse and who wanted to know how to attain the preparation for such winning ways. Second, the response to this appeal was the Holy Spirit's method of showing what is involved in such preparation for such a work of triumph in these times. He is really employing two groups of bystanders, as it were, to bring out His own description of what provides the Lord with a vehicle and the spouse with victory. Thus He engineers one group to make interrogation and the other to make response. In this way there is afforded an opportunity to others of recognizing what the Shulamite experienced in her preparation for the Lord's work. She was now a true Shulamite. Her union with Solomon was inseparable and her identity with Him complete.

The mention of "two armies" refers back to Mahanaim in Genesis 32:2. This was the place where Jacob met God's host. The word "company" should be translated "dance." Hence the answer was given in the form of a dance. The Mahanaim dance must have been as exciting as it was spectacular. You will see from Exodus 15:20 and I Samuel 18:6 that the dance was an expression of victory; and two in the Scripture is the number representing witness or testimony. The sentence may therefore read, "What will ye see in the Shulamite? As it were, a testimony in the dance of victory."

THE WORKMANSHIP OF GOD (7:1-9a)

We now are given the words of this victory-dance song (7:1-5). They tell of her preparation for the work of God by recounting her life and way.

"How beautiful are thy feet with shoes, O prince's daughter!

the joints of thy thighs are like jewels, the work of the hands of a cunning workman" (7:1).

At this point the Holy Spirit spoke through a segment of the bystanders in response to the aforementioned interrogation. Their song makes it clear that the spouse had come into the realization of the Spirit's desire. As she came back into view, this new description of her by this third party began touching upon her walk.

In addressing her as "O prince's daughter" there is a recognition of her descent from nobility and of her high birth from royal line. The reference to "shoes" refers obviously to her having been shod with the "Gospel of peace," as in Ephesians 6:15, and thus shows her readiness for His work. Attention is focused upon this preparation, and the reference to her shoes is thus emphasized. The work of evangelization committed to her was as "jewels" most precious. "Thighs" symbolized strength and spoke of the strength of her witness for Christ with which to do His work. This strength had come to her as the gift of God through years of discipline and training. If our thighs are to be like jewels then they must be as Jacob's thighs. You will recall that the hollow of Jacob's thigh was struck out of joint by the Lord on the night the Lord wrestled with him at Peniel (Genesis 32:25). This was meant to teach him and us that the strength of spiritual performance must forever be derived, not from the strength of the flesh, but from God alone. His work is always the "work of a skilled workman," for God Himself is that Workman.

"Thy navel is like a round goblet, which wanteth not liquor: thy belly is like an heap of wheat set about with lilies" (7:2).

These figures spoke of what she was inwardly. The mixed wine or "liquor" points to the blood of the Lord Jesus and the "heap of wheat" indicates His flesh. In very truth then, she is one who knows the inward satisfaction derived from having partaken of His flesh and blood. This means she has learned how to partake of His life in full measure. The "wheat set about with lilies" denotes that she received the wine and wheat of life with a pure faith.

"Thy two breasts are like two young roes that are twins" (7:3).

This passage does not mention, as before, the feeding of

the roes among the lilies. It is not an inference as to how she grew in grace, but rather, that she was now of such maturity of life that she was able to feed others. Faith and love are the twins indicated, and through the strength and fulness of these she had a ministry by which others could be fed.

"Thy neck is as a tower of ivory" (7:4a).

This is a somewhat different figure than that of 4:4 where her neck is described as the "tower of David"—a kind of armory of weapons. This present description of her neck as a tower has newer features because of her having been subject to further dealings with God. The ivory indicates a suffering process. These sufferings were not a mere passive character, but came about when she was faced with issues which touched her Lord. In such trials she had stood immutable as a tower. The tower of ivory, then, implied that she was prepared for any cost, even to suffer death, in order that the Lord's purpose be realized in her life.

"Thine eyes like the fishpools in Heshbon, by the gate of Bath-rabbim" (7:4b).

Her eyes are not as doves' eyes now but are as the water in a pool. This is different from well water which is lacking in light since it lies deep in darkness—nor is pool water to be compared with the water of a fountain which bubbles up all the time. A pool is open to the light of heaven, suggesting that this loved maiden had a heart before God which was notable for openness and purity. Her heart was not only free from the stirrings of any cloudy content but it was entirely at peace and perfectly reflected the will of God. "Heshbon" means "clever" or "understanding," and "Bath-rabbim" is defined as "a daughter of a large company." Thus the spouse of Christ has a spirit much in advance of the average believer.

"Thy nose is as the tower of Lebanon which looketh toward Damascus" (7:4c).

The nose has not been mentioned before because the sense of smell comes more into prominence when things come to ripeness and fulness. In things spiritual not many have either an acute auditory sense or visionary sense, but they who have developed a sense of smell are truly few and far between. This sense is derived, not from words heard or

actions seen, but from an inner discernment. Such percepti-
bility transcends things seen and heard and is an ability
to distinguish and discriminate between fragrance and evil
odor. It is a spiritual discernment which recognizes what is
of God, not by means of natural rationalization, but by an
inner awareness which is spontaneous and precise. It knows
immediately whether or not a thing has a heavenly origin.
At the same time it recognizes evil savor. Such a believer
may not have the natural ability to point out error in doctrine or pinpoint the reason for another's shortcomings, but
yet there will be this well-developed inner sense by which he
knows that there is something wrong in doctrine and prac-
tice. This is the meaning of the nose. And in that it is "as
the tower of Lebanon which looketh toward Damascus,"
this simply means that it is a sense that is high and pointed,
having its special power of discrimination in the realm which
has to do with the fragrance and purpose of God. The
trouble today is that there are too many flat-nosed Christians
—too many by far.

"Thine head upon thee is like Carmel" (7:5a).

Carmel was the site where Elijah acted for God in the
presence of God. It was the place where he battled with all
that was of Baal and demonstrated the victory of the Lord
over everything false and evil. It was the ground upon
which his mighty prayers were heard and answered by fire
from heaven. Since the spouse had a head like Carmel it
implied, therefore, that the whole mind and heart expressed
the superior knowledge and power of heavenly things and the
ability, such as Elijah had, to lead wayward people back to
God.

**"The hair of thine head like purple; the king is held in the
galleries [tresses]" (7:5b).**

The hair once again refers to an extraordinary dedication.
But here we see a further import of dedication in that it can
captivate and hold the King in its tresses or galleries. The
implication is that such believers as represented by the
spouse take hold of the Lord by this very instrument of subjection so that their petitions cannot lack an answer. In
earlier states of spiritual life such power could not be en-

trusted to her from the Lord, but it was now made possible in that she was wholly delivered from the motivations of selfish interest.

When her dedication of devotion and capacity for obedience had reached maturity, and when her mind had become so filled with the thought and understanding of her Bridegroom's glory, her hair turned purple. The purple, of course, represents throne authority. This verse does not mean that the King was held in any carnal power by His bride to fulfill her own desires, but, rather, that she held Him in such spiritual affections as to fulfill completely His desires and promise. The constant expression of her whole being could be summed up something like this: "I pray Thee, Lord, perfect Thy plan and purpose in me, and do according to Thy Word." She had now learned how to exercise throne authority over others, and this was symbolized in her purple hair.

Then at this point, the Lord Himself broke into the song.

"How fair and how pleasant art thou, O love, for delights!" (7:6).

In the previous verses it was the Holy Spirit speaking through a chorus of the daughters of Jerusalem. What the Holy Spirit had expressed about this loved maiden was precisely and exactly the mind of the Lord Himself. The Lord could continue to speak, therefore, as though it were He who had hitherto been singing right along. As the Lord listened to the descriptive words of the Holy Spirit, up through verse 5, He suddenly and spontaneously broke into the strain, and He Himself pronounced agreement with the Holy Spirit as to the spiritual delights with which the life of the maiden was now enriched.

"This thy stature is like to a palm tree, and thy breasts to clusters of grapes" (7:7).

In the early part of her spiritual experience there had been neither progress nor maturity, and therefore no spiritual stature to speak about. But now the time of maturity was at hand, and thus the Lord was able to speak about stature. The palm tree, to which He likened her stature, is tall and straight. Scripturally speaking, the palm tree is representative of the Lord Himself. The fact that His elect bride was now like a palm tree meant that she had "the measure of the stature of the fulness of Christ" (Ephesians 4:13). The roots of the palm tree are in touch with a deep fountain of living waters. Though exposed to a hot, tropical sunshine, its foliage and fruit grow without hindrance. Thus we are taught that though such believers as this spouse live in a desert world and are subject to fierce trials and testings, yet there is a hidden union with Christ which causes them to blossom and to bear fruit without being affected by the worldly influences to which they are exposed.

"And thy breasts to clusters of grapes." Once again He is referring to her enlarged capacity for feeding others. The breasts are not only for the expression of love but for the purpose of nursing. In the days of her immaturity, the expression of love was paramount, but there was very little capacity to nourish others. Now in her maturity this aspect of her ability to feed others is more manifest. The attention to the breasts in this part focuses upon the very question of feeding, and therefore they are likened to clusters of grapes which are capable of supplying and satisfying the hunger of others.

"I said, I will go up to the palm tree, I will take hold of the boughs thereof: now also thy breasts shall be as clusters of the vine, and the smell of thy nose like apples [citrons]; and the roof of thy mouth like the best wine—" (7:8-9a).

This seems to imply that the Lord had something to take hold of in this mature maiden by reason of her having come to full stature. The Lord purposes to have fellowship with believers, and here it appears as though He is in search of such as this loved one rather than she seeking Him. Having such a spiritual stature and having life and strength in her branches, as it were, He had something to take hold of for fellowship. What a contrast this is to earlier days when she said "I sat down under his shadow" (2:3). Here the Lord mentions three aspects of her mature life which were especially satisfying to Him.

First, her capacity to feed others. "Thy breasts shall be as clusters of the vine." His words about her breasts were words of blessing and expressed the hope of increase so that there would be enlargement of this capacity.

Second, her well-developed sensory organ of smell. "The smell of thy nose like citrons." Attention is directed not so much to a particular organ, but rather to the fact that the scent that is fragrant now exudes from her whole being as a result of her previous contacts and experiences with Him. One has to eat a citron if one is to know the sweetness of the aroma. We know that in Scripture the citron points to Christ, and she, having partaken of Christ, now exuded the very fragrance of His life.

Third, her sensitive and discriminatory taste. "The roof of thy mouth like the best wine." This meant she had a taste for the world to come (Heb. 6:5). The best wine is the millennium to come, as in John 2:10: "thou hast kept the good wine until now"—the wine of the millennial age; as also in Matthew 26:29: "But I say unto you, I will not drink henceforth of this fruit of the vine, until the day when I drink it new with you in my Father's kingdom." This bride was now able to give the Lord a taste of what the millennium will mean to Him.

CO-WORKER WITH THE LORD (7:9b-13)

As the Lord came to this point in His own narration, the bride, being in perfect union with Him, broke in to interrupt Him and to say:

"—like the best wine for my beloved, that goeth down sweetly" (7:9b).

This implied that she and her Beloved together had already tasted something of the supreme blessedness of millennial glory.

"Causing the lips of those that are asleep to speak" (7:9c).

Enjoying the repose of sleep were many others who had similar exalted tastes as had the bride for things spiritual. And here their being "asleep," as in her own case of "sleep" in 5:2, does not signify anything evil or out of order. All who thus sleep are one with the Lord and in the category of believers, for sleep here refers to all those who have found rest in Him from sin and self. It points to all who have lost sympathy with their own soulish life but who have found rest and livingness in the Lord.

"I am my beloved's, and his desire is toward me" (7:10).

Her attention is now focused on the question of what is her Beloved's pleasure. At this stage she has fully renounced her right to herself and the pursuit of selfish interests. If it could be supposed that the Beloved One did not have desire in His heart to possess her, then she was now willing to forfeit Him for the satisfaction of His pleasure. Her primary concern was, "What is my Beloved's desire?" As for her own heart, it has been wholly given to Him, and this spiritual affection for the Lord is her whole heart content. The laying hold of Him in a carnal way for private satisfaction has completely evaporated.

But in the early stages of her life with Him her primary thought was, "My beloved is mine," and it was quite secondary to say "I am his." In this order there was a sense of possessiveness for her personal pleasure, and although later there was some adjustment to this, yet she had never been wholly free from the thought that she had a hold upon Him as a special possession of hers. But now, by reason of the profound exercises of varying dealings and disciplines, we no longer hear that boastful remark of hers, "My beloved is mine," but, rather, the primary expression is, "I am my beloved's." In the quest for spiritual progress there oftentimes exists in the believer a working for personal gain. Who among believers reaches the stage where, in one's devotion to Christ, he no longer suspects a secret lurking of desire merely to satisfy one's own self?

The question at hand, then, is not that of the spouse's personal pleasure but rather that of the Beloved One's own desire. She realizes that she now lives only for His pleasure and to be desired by Him and not to impose herself on Him. To live so as to be desirable to the Lord is the highest purpose of a believer's life. The question is not how I may feel, or what I may gain, or what service I may render, but whether, as a believer, I am desirable to Him. To be able to say "His desire is toward me" is at once the most delightful and satisfying of all spiritual experiences.

When the loved maiden arrived at this position, which she attained only as every form of self-manifestation had been dealt with through an unlimited measure of the Lord's dealings with her, she was made ready to be a co-laborer with her Bridegroom Lover. Being filled with the fulness of His Spirit, she was now able to initiate a work on His behalf. Outwardly, at least, it appeared that she was originating some movement, but in reality the Spirit of the Lord, dwelling in her, was moving and motivating her to this activity. The union with Christ was so complete that her works now had the inspiration and dependability of the divine character. She could therefore say what follows.

"Come, my beloved, let us go forth into the field" (7:11a).

In this going forth to the work she was not now acting alone, nor was the Lord moving in an individualistic way without her. They were moving together into the work. From now on, therefore, one can discern a togetherness in their toil for God. And since the spouse has been set free from all selfish motivations, she is also delivered from that narrowness into which self ever retreats. She is no longer interested in "my meetings," "my work," "my church," "my community," but in the vast total field of the Lord's interests in the world. She possesses world vision, yea, a vision which even transcends the whole world and all things which pertain to the world. To her there is no longer any work which is called her work, nor is there any particular area which is her special sphere. The whole field of the Lord's interests has become her scope of service, and she is one with Him in all of it. Her mind is now occupied with His whole field of operation.

"Let us lodge in the villages" (7:11b).

And "villages," we note, is plural. With her Lord, she now has the nature of a pilgrim in the world. It is not a settled home that she is in quest of, but she realizes that her life with Him is a pilgrim journey. Such a one on such a pilgrimage cannot settle for an abiding place on earth, so she passes with Him from village to village. As she thus journeys in His company, she follows Him in His quest for lost or maimed sheep. And thus we see that in becoming a co-laborer with the Lord, not only must one have total world vision of His interests, but one must constantly preserve the reality and character of a pilgrim.

"Let us get up early to the vineyards" (7:12a).

Here she draws attention not to her own personal vineyard but to a plurality of vineyards beyond herself. Her concern and burden are now extended to many works of the Lord. In the beginning of any service for the Lord, believers must learn not to yield to the temptation of working in too many vineyards, but, rather, to cultivate one's own vineyard. Remember the loved maiden's lament in her immaturity: "They made me the keeper of the vineyards; but mine own vineyard have I not kept" (1:6). But now she had been brought to spiritual maturity through caring for, and giving attention to, the development of the ground in her own life.

Having been released from all selfish motivations in doing works for the Lord, she is now capable of caring for many vineyards. The whole of the Lord's work is now her burden, and not merely that of some specific work entrusted to her. Whatever, therefore, is done for Him in any vineyard finds her with a portion of concern for its welfare. I do not say that she has lost her individual touch in some specific work. It is rather, I would say, that she has come to a sense of corporate responsibility with all the Lord's servants for His work in many vineyards. This is something which can be spoken only to one who has first learned to care for and cultivate his own vineyard.

"Let us get up early." This indicates her industrious character. In the work of the Lord the early morning exercises are of utmost importance. Laziness is no characteristic of spiritual life, and only the truly spiritual man can be diligent and industrious before the Lord. There are some forms of activity which spring forth from the natural life and are not to be confused with spiritual exercises. There also are works which arise from the principle of self-interest and which are unacceptable to Him. Every form of fleshly activity must be resolutely resisted, whether it be the extreme busyness of mere natural drive and dynamic or the more passive form which issues in laziness and lack of responsibility. In either form, these works of the flesh must be laid aside. The difference between industriousness of a spiritual character and spiritual slothfulness lies in the use of time. We are to redeem the time because the days are evil, and such is the command of the apostle in Ephesians 5:16.

The loved maiden now went down with her Beloved to the vineyards to

"see if the vine flourish, whether the tender grape appear, and the pomegranates bud forth" (7:12b).

Their attention was focused upon the phenomenon of life as they searched for the signs of fruitage. Now that she had been set free from self-consideration, her mind was captivated with interest and concern for all the Lord's work and the growth of life in every believer, as she moves with her Lord. Even the smallest measure of life in the youngest and most tender plants drew her interest. The question uppermost in the mind of those who are represented by the spouse is not who shall be leaders or whether believers belong to one's own particular meeting, but *how to bring Christ to His people*. This type of work-fellowship can only come after a complete union with the Lord.

"There will I give thee my loves [caresses]" (7:12c).

And what, may we ask, does "there" mean? It points to the whole range of the Lord's interests in the fields, the villages, and the vineyards. It is an outlook upon the whole wide domain of His work in the world. It is in such a sphere that she is now able to give Him her loves. She can manifest her love to Him in His work. It is in such a sphere that she is now able to show Him her love. How wonderful this is! In former days, work was a detraction to her love. Service cumbered her as it did Martha and drew her away from that fellowship of love which Mary enjoyed at His feet. Her early experience of service not only prevented any full expression of devotion, but became the originating cause of estrangement from her Beloved. Such issues were the natural phenomena of incomplete union. But now that she had entered into a place of complete devotion she was enabled to link together the Lord and His work, to join together the Lord and His people, and to bring different brethren into harmonious relationship to the Lord. It was this area of service where she could now express her love to Christ and most manifest His working in her. By means of this elevated spiritual service she was now able to give Him her loves. In such works she no longer carried feelings of guilt which made her fear that somehow and somewhere she may have turned away from Him and lost His fellowship.

"The mandrakes give a smell" (7:13a).

Mandrake is a love plant and, as in Genesis 30:14-16, signifies the most intimate union between husband and wife. In such a state as attained by the spouse at this stage of her spiritual life, what could she say but that this union with her Beloved gave forth every kind of fragrance. She had reached completion of the love union with Him.

"And at our gates are all manner of pleasant fruits, new and old, which I have laid up for thee, O my beloved" (7:13b).

The gates point to what was near at hand. Although her interests roamed through many villages and vineyards, this did not imply that she herself had to go far distances to gather fruit. Whatever was her assigned vocation from the Lord, there were fruits to glean right there.

Her attention, too, we note, was awakened to quite a variety of fruits. Prior to her deliverance from a life of self-consideration she could not perceive any fruit in any believer unless it bore her own particular brand mark. She now sees that pleasant fruits are of vast variety and not of one species only. There also were new fruits and old. Thus she had a developed spirit of discernment to differentiate what is new and what is old. Different believers brought forth different kinds of fruit, and this was a truth which now became very clear to her. The company of those who receive the Lord Jesus is very large and although but one company, and that company a new creation, yet all in that company did not bear the same fruit. The fruit of the Spirit is manifold: "love, joy, peace, longsuffering, gentleness, goodness, faith, meekness, temperance" (Gal. 5:22-23). The total harvest of such fruits is for the Lord's own praise and glory. And we are to remember, too, that the fruit of service, as that of character, is not for self-glorification. We are indeed the Lord's co-laborers, but the glory of the harvest is the Lord's.

PART FIVE (8:1-14)

MATURE LOVE

GROANING FOR BODILY RELEASE (8:1-4)

This last section of the Song begins with the spouse's longing for deliverance from the bondage and groaning of the physical nature (8:1-4). As the believer grows into deeper union with Christ, as in the case of this loved maiden, there is an increasing realization that the presence of the outer man or carnal shell imposes limitation upon the spirit within. The inner man is renewed daily but the outer man decays day by day. The corruptible body of flesh is kept for its allotted period by the revivings and refreshments of the Holy Spirit, but it must needs die. The power of God is often displayed through its weakness, yet the body of flesh remains very much as a thorn in the side of the spirit.

Thus, as the believer increases in spiritual affections and develops into maturity, he is made conscious that final perfection is still curtailed by the present limitations of the flesh. Even though the believer has borne the first-fruits of resurrection life in his inner man, yet he is not exempted from that groaning within which is echoed by the whole creation. "For we know that the whole creation groaneth and travaileth in pain together until now. And not only they, but ourselves also, which have the firstfruits of the Spirit, even we ourselves groan within ourselves, waiting for the adoption, to wit, the redemption of our body" (Romans 8:22-23).

During the time a believer lives in the strength of the flesh, there is no awareness of need for the redemption of the body. It is only as union with Christ becomes a fuller reality that believers begin to distinguish the difference between the outward body and the inner man. If the body is not altogether a hindrance, it is at best a very great weakness, and, in an advanced state of spiritual maturity, the necessity for bodily redemption becomes an all-important phase of grace.

"O that thou wert as my brother, that sucked the breasts of my mother! when I should find thee without, I would kiss thee; yea, I should not be despised" (8:1).

In ancient Israel public kissing between men and women, even by husband and wife, was considered a breach of the standards of decency. The only exception allowed was between blood-relatives, such as brother and sister. Hence the maiden felt restrained, and unable to display adequately to the world the reality of His loveliness and the depth of her love for Him. So in effect she was saying: "Oh, that Thou wert my brother! — that there could be a full manifestation of the complete oneness of our relationship in God, so that when I publicly acknowledge and express my love to Thee, my Beloved, I should not be despised and ridiculed by others as being indiscreetly affectionate.

"While this state of existence here in the body persists, I am very aware of my inability to be unto Thee all I should be and that the despisings of others restrain my affections. In the beginning my sole desire was for Thee to kiss me so that I could glory in Thy love as my own possession. But now it is I who desire to kiss Thee. I would continually express my love to Thee and seek to satisfy Thine heart with my love. The chief hindrance to this full expression of my affections is my earth-boundness. While I remain in this body, the full manifestation of utter oneness of nature, as that of a brother, cannot as yet be realized. I am ever under the conviction, therefore, that I do not serve Thee as I ought."

"I would lead thee, and bring thee into my mother's house, who would instruct me: I would cause thee to drink of spiced wine of the juice of my pomegranate" (8:2).

So she continues something like this: "When that day of perfect liberty comes, it will be most necessary, my Beloved, to lead Thee into that Jerusalem above, which is the mother of us all (the system of grace, as in Gal. 4:26), so that I may learn to express perfectly the great doctrine of grace. I will then know that nothing is owing to the flesh—not a thing.

"I must have final deliverance, therefore, from this body of flesh so that not even this unglorified flesh shall have part in my praise. Then all the spiritual fruit which my life has borne shall be pressed into a fragrant wine to fill up Thine own cup of delight. The spiritual fruit given by Thee shall not have one iota of fleshly glory, nor shall there be the least thing for my personal satisfaction. All the pomegranates of today, so full of seed, shall then be turned into a sweet and fragrant wine for Thine own heart's satisfaction. When I am made free from the last vestiges of the flesh, I shall then offer Thee my all, and all shall be for Thy delight throughout the ages of eternity."

"His left hand should be under my head, and his right hand should embrace me" (8:3).

Here she is saying: "On that blessed day of final deliverance from earthly limitations I will be in Thy full embrace. Thy left hand will be under my head steadying me to look constantly into Thy face. Thy right hand will hold me in such loving embrace that I shall be able to behold Thee face to face as I lie nearest Thine heart and in Thy bosom. Such a day, my Beloved, is the desire of my heart. Oh, that that day would come soon."

"I charge you, O daughters of Jerusalem, that ye stir not up, nor awake my love, until he please" (8:4).

The virgin spouse now dwells on the hope of her Lord's return and of being soon taken up to be with Him forever. Her feelings are ecstatic, and these are now legitimate and right by reason of her full and mature affections. It is a state of blessed anticipation and the fruit of her long spiritual exercise. She would not have others disturb this blessed anticipation or interfere, with any stretched-out hand of flesh, so as to disrupt her spiritual life again until she rises into His glorious presence.

PREPARATION FOR THE SECOND COMING
(8:5-14)

Then, finally, we view her as just prior to the rapture in verses 5-14.

"Who is this that cometh up from the wilderness, leaning upon

her beloved? I raised thee up under the apple tree: there thy mother brought thee forth: there she brought thee forth that bare thee" (8:5).

Twice in the Song mention is made of her coming up from the wilderness. The first reference in 3:6 was at the commencement of her union with the Lord. There followed a renunciation of herself for the Lord. Then came the desire to live altogether in the life of the Lord. Finally, she went on to dwell in all the blessings of grace bestowed by the Lord.

From that point onward she made constant and considerable progress, and as she went forward she began to leave behind that kind of poor spiritual life represented by the figure of a wilderness. In moving out of this desert kind of life there were occasions when she stalled or faltered in her step for a little while. We would not say that such haltings were necessary or inevitable, but we would dare to say that such were forgivable. Her life of spiritual wanderlust had been abandoned forever because of her deep and vital union with her Beloved. Her step was forward with her Lord in all His goings. We must now enquire, therefore, why the Spirit once again makes mention of her coming up from the wilderness. It appears at first glance as though all her intervening history took place while she was still in a spiritual wilderness.

It is worthy of attention, therefore, to understand just what this wilderness signifies. We know well from personal experience that one of our wildernesses is a life marked by spiritual poverty and wandering. But another is the world in which we meet so many trials and disciplines. The one is in the realm of the spirit; the other in the physical world, which brings its pressures from many areas.

As we find deliverance from the wilderness of inward spiritual wandering, so also we may find like freedom from the outward power and pressures of the world around us. For when the Holy Spirit takes complete control of us through His indwelling presence, then we experience deliverance, not only from the wilderness within but from the wilderness without. It is the Cross of Christ which delivers us from the spiritual wilderness, and it is the call of His return which delivers us from our wandering through, and the holdings of, the present world — for the promise of His return summons us to readiness.

The Holy Spirit again employs the method of interrogation through a third party. "Who is this that cometh up from the wilderness?" He pictures to us the maiden coming up from the wilderness, leaning harder and harder upon her Beloved. As she proceeds she comes clearer and clearer into vision and focus. The question He asks is: "Who is she?" This is meant to excite a very clear reply from the Beloved One Himself.

One thing is clear in this picture, namely that the call and influence of His return extend over a period of time. It is this call which inspires the loved maiden to leave the world behind by a step by step walk with the Lord. Thus we see that the revelation and reality of Christ's return in the life of the believer begins when such a one is drawn away from the world and, under the compulsion of a heavenly destiny, leaves it behind. The face then is set toward a heavenly goal; the back is given to the world. This maiden is not of the world, but turns from all its appeals to a closer and yet closer union with her Lord. This is precisely how Enoch was prepared for his translation. We must never imagine that the sudden event of the Lord's return and our translation will effect any sudden change in our spiritual condition. It is spiritual fitness which makes us ready for His return, and this demands a close walk with the Lord.

The present, then, is a time for preparation, and the best preparation is that which is seen in this maiden as she comes more and more out from the world and leans closer and closer upon the Beloved. This is a recognition that in herself she is wholly without strength and needs His support for such a walk. "Leaning upon her beloved" implies that she is a burden to be borne, but she finds restful support upon the strong shoulders of her Beloved. She is "leaning upon her beloved" as though, like Jacob of old, the hollow of her thigh (her natural strength) is out of joint and unable to provide any pillar to lean upon. "Leaning upon her beloved" also suggests that she is incapable of finding her own paths out from this wilderness world, and thus she must cleave to her Beloved. Indeed, it is only the Lord Himself who can lead a believer into fitness for the final redemption so that "the life of trust is a must" in preparation for the great event. With a sense of utter helplessness in ourselves we must constantly lean upon the Lord Jesus until it is asked with a true sense of amazement: "Who is this . . . leaning upon her beloved?"

The question brings forth a clear description of her by the Beloved One. "I raised thee up under the apple tree: there thy mother brought thee forth: there she brought thee forth that bare thee." She is none other than a poor sinner sought by grace, discovered by grace, and saved by grace. And this grace, the "Jerusalem which is above . . . which is the mother of us all" (Galatians 4:26), includes the Father's eternal plan and divine election, the whole redemptive work of His eternal Son, and the sanctifying processes of His Holy Spirit. Grace is the whole work of the Triune God as recorded in His Holy Word. When that grace seeks out a sinner, such a one is placed under the overshadowing of the Saviour, who commends His love and travails for that one until life is given, and that one rises up into the reality of the love of Christ.

The apple or citron tree here is the same as in 2:3 and is a figure of Christ in the fulness of His love. When the eyes of this maiden were first opened they opened upon Him, who is "altogether lovely," and the first thing she discovered was that there is sustenance and security in the shadow of His love. It was in her discovery of Him as "the apple tree among the trees of the wood" that she found her true self and reached her spiritual zenith. How good and beneficial it was for her now to be reminded by the Beloved of her origin in grace! She was entirely and altogether indebted to Him and to His grace.

"Set me as a seal upon thine heart, as a seal upon thine arm: for love is strong as death; jealousy is cruel as the grave: the coals thereof are coals of fire, which hath a most vehement flame" (8:6).

After the reminder of her true origin she could not help but cherish deep feelings of humility. She would be conscious of her own nothingness, the fruitlessness of her own efforts, her undependable aspirations, and the unrewarding search on her part for anything of value. Now all her hope was focused upon the Lord Himself, for if she were to keep on to the end, then it would certainly never be by her own persistence but by the Lord's own keeping and sustaining power. Not even all the spiritual edification of others could be sufficient means of persistent progress, but only the Lord's own constant grace and power.

Having come to the realization of this truth she now had to say: "Set me as a seal upon thine heart, as a seal upon thine arm." The "heart" is the seat of love and the "arm" is where strength lies. She was thus requesting the Lord to give her a permanent place in His heart and to make her conscious of His firm security. In effect she was saying: "Just as the priests of old carried the names of the tribes of Israel in their breastplates upon their shoulders, so I entreat Thee, hold me close to Thine heart and sustain me with the strength of Thine arm. I know my frailty and my proneness to vanity. I am conscious of my helplessness.

"Oh Lord, for me to try to keep myself until I see Thy face would only spell shame to Thy Name and bring about my own loss and failure. All my hope for continuance rests upon Thine own love and power. In the past I have professed love of Thee, but how unreliable that love proved to be! Now I look only to Thee. At one time I held fast Thine hand (3:4), and though my grip was naturally strong yet how weak it was to hold on to Thee! My own strength was utter weakness, so that today my trust no longer rests in strength of my own. Thy love and power must forever hold me. I dare no longer make mention even of my love to Thee, but only of Thine to me."

"For love is strong as death," and who can cause death to be shaken of its hold? The sighs of parents, the tears of a wife, the heartache of friends, none of these can overcome the strength of death. Death watches over its victims and holds them in a vice unshakeable and immovable. "If Thou lovest me, then I shall be stablished forever, for Thy love can never be weakened by death, and Thou canst never lose Thine hold upon me. Since Thou lovest me, then Thy holy jealousy will follow hard after me, for 'jealousy is cruel as the grave.' If Thou dost chastise me, then it will be for keeping whole my love, since Thou wouldest not permit anything to estrange my heart from Thee. The more Thou hast of me, the stronger will be Thy hold upon me, for Thou wouldest not part with any of me. Thine eyes would not suffer Thy loved one to be tainted with the world or to be taken by another love.

"So, I am wholly Thine; then jealous Thou wouldest be, for since time immemorial Thou art a jealous God (Exodus 20:5). Yea, have not Thine own blessed apostles instructed us in godly jealousy when Paul said, 'I am jealous over you with godly jealousy' (II Corinthians 11:2). If Thou art jealous then what in me can resist Thy jealousy? Thou wilt destroy all Thine enemies and remove every impediment to our union of love until Thou art the Lord supreme to me and thus possess me without a rival. Then only, my Beloved, shall I be kept by Thee as a chaste spouse until I see Thee face to face.

"Thy jealousy, Lord, I know, is cruel as the grave. And what could be more cruel? When the grave takes the most lovely, or precious, or hardest to part with, it is unmoved by any appeal by others on the grounds that the one in the grave may be lovely, or precious, or hard to part with. Tears can never move the grave. Neither sorrow nor pleading can change its intention. The grave recognizes no companion, no pity, no sympathy, no feeling. It is, in a sense, a cruel grave. And if I offer Thee myself as a chaste spouse to be Thine and Thine alone, and if Thou dost find in me that love which causes to arise in Thee a holy jealousy, then Thou wilt guard my love, though it might have to set aside and at naught the persuasion of loved ones, or the pleading of friends, or the tears of some dear ones. But only by Thine own jealous guardianship shall I be kept secure.

" 'The coals thereof are coals of fire, which hath a most vehement flame.' Thou art, my Lord Jehovah, a consuming fire (Hebrews 12:29). Thy love to me, and Thy jealousy over me, are as a vehement flame or as a flash of fire which burns up all that is valueless and combustible, all that is of time and corruptible, all that is of the world and is mortal and temporary.

" 'Many waters cannot quench love, neither can the floods drown it: if a man would give all the substance of his house for love, it would utterly be contemned' (8:7).

"Thy love, Lord, with its flame of divine fire, cannot be quenched by the 'many waters' of trials and testings, nor by the 'floods' which pour forth from a persecuting enemy. Neither trials nor persecutions can do anything to prevent Thy love to me. Such love as Thine cannot be purchased nor can there be found any substitute.

"Neither the tongues of men nor of angels have any value apart from Thy love. Neither the gift of prophecy, nor the understanding of all mysteries, nor the acquiring of all knowledge, nor the possession of all faith, is a sufficient exchange for Thine own dear love. Though I were to give all my goods to feed the poor and my body to be burned, they are to be utterly despised as a substitute for Thy love. Such things are comparable only to the treasures of a household, but are not to be compared or exchanged for the reality of Thy great love. Thus, O my Lord, I have not sought to win Thy love by means of increased service, or by more time spent in Thy service, or even by reinforced dedication. I can only offer myself as a living sacrifice unto Thee, who first loved me, and thus offer myself to be one who is just to be loved by Thee."

"We have a little sister, and she hath no breasts: what shall we do for our sister in the day when she shall be spoken for?" (8:8).

We see in this spouse, then, one who dwells fully in the love of Christ. She could not help but remember the fact that there were others who would like to enjoy such love. Before she herself had come through to the realized presence of the Lord and so to behold His face, her great concern had been over the immaturity of other believers. Now in His presence, therefore, she mentions her "little sister," by which she means those believers in whom there is a measure of life but very much immaturity in faith and love towards Him. Because of her own complete union with the Lord, she is now able to pour out her heart's concern directly to Him about this matter. "What shall we do," is her burden, "for our sister in the day when she shall be spoken for?"

This immature sister had come to see in the spouse an example of a true life of love. And she had hope that the Eternal Lover would, by means of the Holy Spirit's energy and work, lead her into the same kind of love union and fellowship. In view of her desire, what could be done for her? Regarding her measure of life and her spiritual development, she was but a little sister. The fact that her breasts were undeveloped indicated a lack of maturity in spiritual stature and affections. Believers such as these demand the loving concern of the more mature, for no undeveloped state of spiritual love can give the Lord any satisfaction at all. In the life of every believer there comes a day when such a one is spoken for, and appealed to, by the Lord. To respond or not to respond rests in one's liberty to choose. But there is no exception to the rule that the Lord requires a full growth of love and faith in each believer. The question arises, therefore, how can we help our little sister and remedy such an undeveloped condition?

Thus burdened with the immature state of others, the spouse now communes with her Beloved about it. She herself is so much in the will of God that she can use the familiar "we." Her concern was now so much in unity with the Lord's mind that she could say "we." What she desired Him to do was exactly what the Lord wanted to do; therefore she said "we." She was so completely in union and harmony with her Beloved that her prayer was no longer petition, but, rather, an expression of what God's will was for this little sister. This desire of the spouse for less-developed believers was not at all motivated by any selfish interest, nor was it the exercise of a condescending spirit; but rather it was the pure expression of what was the united desire of both her Beloved and herself — and the reply of her Beloved shows that this was so:

"If she be a wall, we will build upon her a palace of silver: and if she be a door, we will inclose her with boards of cedar" (8:9).

If there be in her something that is truly of God and thus something which makes her different and separated from all that is not of God, as a wall would suggest, then there is ground upon which can be built "a palace of silver." There can be constructed upon her life all that is derived from redemption and all that is high and noble. If she is indeed living a life separated unto God through the presence and power of the Holy Spirit, then her life can be built up with the fruits of redemption.

"If she be a door," that is, if she is indeed such a witness that others may enter by her into the true knowledge of God, then we will build into her the new heavenly life of Christ whose "countenance is as the cedar." "We" — that is, I with the help of your example (I Corinthians 11:1). They both desired nothing but the best for this little sister.

"I am a wall, and my breasts like towers: then was I in his eyes as one that found favour [peace]" (8:10).

She views herself as one that is set apart for the Lord Himself. He had brought her forth from all that which was unclean, worldly, and common. Her remark about her breasts was an attestation that her faith and love, dependent upon separation from the world for their development, had grown to full maturity. The Lord had built up these and strongly established them in her. These virtues were no longer unformed, but they rose high like towers in their prominence. Thus she was in His sight as one who found favor and peace. She had become one who had begun to enjoy a true life of peace. We see from this that separation is the foundation of such a life and that true peace issues from maturity of faith and love. This was her testimony given in a figure of great simplicity, and utterly free from any shadow of self-sufficiency or self-satisfaction. She might have boasted how strong a wall she had become, or how well-developed her breasts were. But no! She merely makes the simple statement that she was now, in the eyes of her Beloved, as one that had found favor.

"Solomon had a vineyard at Baal-hamon; he let out the vineyard unto keepers; every one for the fruit thereof was to bring a thousand pieces of silver" (8:11).

Here is a facet of truth to which the Holy Spirit would direct the attention of believers before the Lord's return. It is the handing out of rewards according to the degree of labor. Solomon had a vineyard, and he let it out to keepers. This vineyard of his represents the whole work of the Lord. It is never our work, but we do have responsibilities in the field as keepers or stewards. We are to keep watch over the Lord's interests. When He returns, all that is entrusted to us is still His own.

"Baal-hamon" means "the Lord of a multitude." Such was Solomon; thus, in fulfilment of the type, so is the Lord Jesus Christ. He is the Lord and Master of many servants. Solomon's rule was that the fruits of the vineyard went to the keepers, so that according to their labor they partook of the fruits. Thus we are to till, plant, keep, prune, and nurture the Lord's ground and plants, and He will presently reward such keepers with the increase of the fruits. What is done for Him is never in vain. Even the giving of a cup of cold water shall have its reward.

"A thousand pieces of silver," however, were required from each keeper, and this they were to bring to the king. This represents increase for the Lord. It is somewhat different from the parables of Matthew 25 and Luke 19. There the return demanded from the servants is related to the number of talents and pounds entrusted to them. These thousand pieces represent what is due to the Lord Himself and what He would receive if the believer worked with fulness of faith and love. When we stand at last before the judgment seat of Christ, we shall learn that the Lord's minimum portion is that which comes from a full and mature Christian life.

"My vineyard, which is mine, is before me: thou, O Solomon, must [shall] have a thousand, and those that keep the fruit thereof two hundred" (8:12).

She now singled out herself from the company of many. She was not an ordinary keeper among Solomon's many vineyard keepers. Solomon had given her a vineyard for her own personal use. This vineyard was now before her and belonged to her; she could do as she pleased with it (Genesis 13:9). Each ordinary keeper was under bond to turn in that increase to Solomon which was represented by the thousand pieces. Out of pure affection this maiden also met the claim. And should love's affection give less than the law's demand? Not so! She paid out of love that which was her measure of responsibility.

We recognize in this thought two forms of service. One

is labor under law; the other, the expression of love. One arises from fear; the other from appreciation. One springs from a sense of duty; the other, from the sheer joy of serving the Lord. Because she now stood on a higher level of spiritual life and had a closer and more intimate relationship with the Beloved, her service was altogether different from that of the great number who served the Lord. Many do Him service from convictions of duty. The loved maiden served out of love, yet her service never fell beneath the demand required by duty.

Not only Solomon profited from this kind of service, but those who kept watch over the fruits were also profitably employed. That is, all workers who assisted in any way in gathering the fruits, were given some credit by her. She did not rob them of that praise which was their due. They had labored too; and in the measure they had done so, she honored them with what was rightfully theirs. Thus she did not encroach upon the glory due to other co-laborers — something all God's servants do well to heed.

But in the day when the Lord comes to reward His servants, she herself would be included among those who kept watch over the fruits and thus receive "two hundred" pieces of silver. The portion for keepers, according to verse 11, was the fruits only, not the silver. But here was a maiden who did not commercialize His reward and pay merely according to law or by the amount of work done. So He gave her over and above what was due her in fruits. He added silver of His own. He bestowed glory upon her. The question at the judgment seat of Christ will be, as in the parables of Matthew and Luke, how we have used the talents and pounds entrusted to us. But here love is brought into focus. It is not a matter of doing our duty or meeting our obligations. Indeed, the question of work and reward should not have been mentioned here. It is another subject, but not for this book. The Holy Spirit calls attention to our service, not from the standpoint of obligation, but from the viewpoint of love, and this agrees perfectly with the character of the Song.

"Thou that dwellest in the gardens, the companions hearken to thy voice: cause me to hear it" (8:13).

The plural "gardens" recognizes that the Lord does not

dwell exclusively in *her* garden (6:2). He dwells in *many* gardens, since He is Lord in the hearts of all His people. He not only dwells where spiritual affections have come to maturity, but in all in whom He is well pleased. She, therefore, capitalizes on this thought in her address to Him: "The companions hearken to thy voice!"

This attitude implies the art of listening. There are others who had assumed an attitude similar to hers in listening to the Beloved. They, too, had experienced His dealings with them, and they had learned well the futility of much talking. They had learned that it was more profitable to listen. Having become familiar with His teaching, they were now swift to hear and slow to speak. Both they and she were no longer as talkative as they used to be in recounting their relationship and experiences with the Lord. They were now different from those who talk for the sake of talking and those who make themselves vocal over trifles because so much of earth occupies their attention.

It is not as before. They now assume a listening attitude. They have come to realize that as their growth in life depends upon the teaching of the Lord, so the prosperity of their work rests upon the personal directives of the Lord. They must not again move — nor, indeed, can they move — without the voice of the Lord. Without that voice being heard there is no revelation of His will, no light upon the path, no knowledge of His ways. The whole life of the believer depends upon what is heard from the Lord. "Therefore, O my Lord, while we wait before Thee with inclined ears, cause me to hear Thy voice! Since Thou hast said, 'Ask, and it shall be given you; seek, and ye shall find; knock, and it shall be opened unto you' (Matthew 7:7), then I beg that Thou wilt cause me to hear. So shall I really hear. Unless Thy Word comes with clear and living tones, what good will I be if I do not hear? Cause me, O my Lord, to hear Thy voice, for this alone will lead me forward until the day of Thy return!" We see, then, that this loved one has learned her lessons well, so that she closes her spiritual career with the utterance of a profound prayer.

"Make haste, my beloved, and be thou like to a roe or to a young hart upon the mountains of spices" (8:14).

What she breathes forth here is identical with her appeal in 2:17, where a similar prayer is recorded. These two appeals, however, have to do with totally different incidents. Hitherto we have noticed the mention of two wildernesses. So now we see mention of two returns (2:17 and 8:14) like a roe or young hart upon the mountains.

We might say the first appeal for His return in 2:17 refers to a return to fellowship. She had lost that. Darkness had settled down on her soul in those days because of a lack of response. She then cried out for a restored communion so that the shadows round her life would flee away. She thus pleaded with Him to come over the mountains of Bether, or separation.

In the present verse the urgent cry for Him to come to her has to do with His Second Coming which is still in the future, and may be very soon. The emphasis here is not on a restored fellowship but on His coming again, which will bring into manifestation the phenomena of His kingdom. Thus it is no longer the mountains of Bether which are mentioned but the mountains of spices. This is a figure of the new millennial world of fragrance and beauty.

At this point her experience was like a drop of water losing itself in the ocean, mingling deeper and ever deeper with the love of Christ. There seems to be little left in the realm of earth but her physical body. Her heart's affections are in another world. Little wonder, therefore, that she cries out with urgency, "Make haste, my Beloved! As the roe or young hart lights upon the mountains of spices, so do Thou descend into Thy glorious kingdom. Although full and mature my love for Thee has now become, yet there remains something more which can be satisfied only by Thy coming. Then shall faith become sight, and prayer shall be praise forever. Love shall then reach its climax and be freed from the shadows of cloud. Then shall I serve and worship before Thee in a sinless state. What a day that will be! So Lord Jesus, make haste! Come quickly!"

AMEN! EVEN SO, COME, LORD JESUS!
AND UNTIL THAT GLORIOUS DAY,
MAY MY GARDEN CONTINUALLY BEAR ITS FRUIT
FOR THE DELIGHT OF *THY* HEART.

This book was produced by the Christian Literature Crusade. We hope it has been helpful to you in living the Christian life. CLC is a literature mission with ministry in over 40 countries worldwide. If you would like to know more about us, or are interested in opportunities to serve with a faith mission, we invite you to write to:

Christian Literature Crusade
P.O. Box 1449
Fort Washington, PA 19034